Heathrow: The first 25 years

Love it or loath it, Heathrow is arguably the most famous airport in the world. Over its 70-year history, Heathrow has always courted controversy; indeed its very foundation was shrouded in subterfuge. Today it has evolved into the busiest international gateway in Europe, a thriving and powerful metropolis within a metropolis, lying inside the boundaries of Greater London.

But it wasn't always that way. Back in 1946, the first commercial services out of Heathrow were famously served by a primitive tented city and passengers braved the elements as they made their way across duckboards towards aircraft often based on converted World War Two bombers. The ensuing 25 years saw Heathrow grow in size and importance as commercial aviation revolutionised the world. Propliners, such as Constellations and Stratocruisers, gave way to turboprops, before the all-conquering sleek new generation of jets roared into existence and changed our lives forever. The future of British civil aviation became inextricably linked with Heathrow, where the likes of the all-powerful BOAC and BEA flew the national flag. This was a golden age of civil aviation, a time when spectators were actively encouraged to watch these monsters as they clawed their way into the skies. As aircraft evolved, so did the airport and new terminals and infrastructure were built. By the 1970s, Heathrow had become the undisputed gateway to Europe and Britain at last had a world-class airport to be proud of. **Allan Burney**

AVIATION ARCHIVE SERIES

The 'golden age' of Heathrow Airport (1945-1970) is the fascinating subject for No 27 in the Aviation Archive series. At its heart lies unparalleled photographic coverage of historic Heathrow, featuring many exclusive and rare shots that have never been published before. As ever, the words and photographs are complemented by 'period' cutaways from the talented pens of the 'Flight' and 'Aeroplane' artists of the era, together with specially-commissioned profiles.

Bibliography: *BOAC: An illustrated history* by Charles Woodley; *Heathrow Airport: The first 25 years* by Charles Woodley; *Heathrow: From tents to Terminal 5* by Ian Anderson; *Time Flies: The Heathrow story* by Alan Gallop; *The Challenge of BEA* by Garry May; *Heathrow: A celebration of 50 years* by BAA.

Aviation Archive Series

Heathrow: The first 25 years

- **Editor:** Allan Burney • **Design:** Key Studio
- **Publisher and Managing Director:** Adrian Cox • **Executive Chairman:** Richard Cox • **Commercial Director:** Ann Saundry • **Group Editor:** Nigel Price
- **Distribution:** Seymour Distribution Ltd +44 (0)20 7429 4000 • **Printing:** Warners (Midlands) PLC, The Maltings, Manor Lane, Bourne, Lincs PE10 9PH.

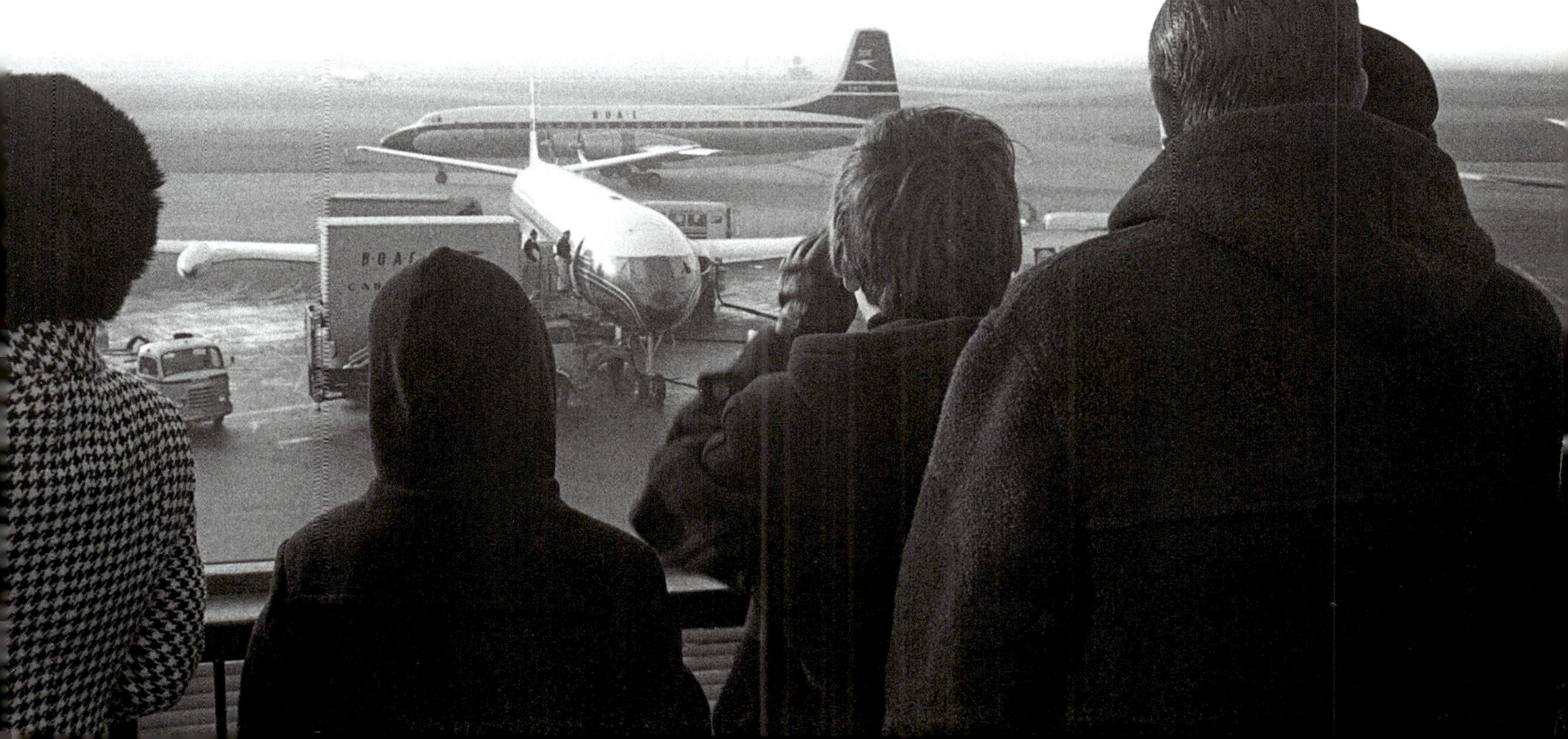

Heathrow: The first 25 years

Tents for terminals

Today, Heathrow is one of the world's busiest international airports handling over 70 million passengers every year. It is used by over 80 airlines flying to 185 destinations in 84 countries. It has four passenger terminals (numbered 2 to 5) and a cargo terminal. It is a city within a city, a pulsating metropolis that never sleeps, beating to the rhythms of commercial aviation. It is exotic, vibrant and a technological masterpiece. As Britain's gateway to the world it reigns supreme. And yet just 70 years ago, the picture could not have been any more different, when tents and converted wartime bombers greeted the adventurous travellers...

Heathrow's place in aviation history can be traced back to World War One when the Army used nearby Hounslow Heath as a training aerodrome for the Royal Flying Corps. In response to the threat of bombs from Zeppelin airships, a crescent of aerodromes was built around the south of London, of which Hounslow Heath became the headquarters. It remained a military airfield until 1919, when it became the first 'Customs' airport for London. In the early 1920s, Hounslow Heath lost this lead in civil aviation to the airport at Croydon, but its links with aviation continued in 1930 when British aero engineer and aircraft builder Richard Fairey paid the Vicar of Harmondsworth £15,000 for a 150-acre plot to build a private

airport to assemble and test aircraft. Complete with a single grass runway and a handful of hastily erected buildings, Fairey's Great West Aerodrome was the humble precursor to the world's busiest international airport, Heathrow.

During World War Two, the search began for a military aerodrome suitable for long-term expansion, able to function as the supply base for the Tiger Force (the RAF's bomber force for the war in the Far East), and of handling the new longer-range, military transport aircraft. Pressure was also mounting to find a new site for London's civil airport. Croydon was considered inappropriate for future expansion, being built on a hill and surrounded by urban sprawl. In October 1943,

Above: The first fare paying passengers to depart from Heathrow on a scheduled BOAC flight walk out towards their aircraft on the wet and blustery morning of 28 May 1946, three days before the airport's official opening. The Lancastrian was flying on the 'kangaroo route' operated jointly by BOAC and Qantas.

a proposal came before Lord Beaverbrook's War Cabinet Committee on Civil Air Transport. The secretary of state for air, Sir Archibald Sinclair, suggested that the Great West Aerodrome might be considered, and developed in several stages, eventually to include the Perry Oaks sewage works (now the site of Terminal 5). The following month, the Lord President's Council, under the deputy prime minister Clement

Atlee, recommended the 'approach in principle to the development of the 'Heath Row' site as a main terminal airport, with its initial use by RAF Transport Command'. According to the plans, all troops and reinforcements for the Far East were to take-off from the new base. At the end of 1943, a Cabinet Committee decided that London's new post-World War Two airport should be Heathrow. Speaking about the decision, civil aviation minister Lord Winster said: 'The site is only 12 miles from the centre of London. The land is remarkably level and the gravel sub-soil has excellent bearing and drainage qualities... To meet the need for a major air terminal to serve London, 52 sites were surveyed. No better site for the

purpose could be found than Heathrow... One of the reasons that led to the siting of the London Airport in this district was that it could be done with the minimum disturbance to house-holders.'

Travelling from his home in Sunningdale to his office in Victoria, British Overseas Airways Corporation (BOAC) director-general Brig Gen A. C. Critchley had also noted the flat open land at Heathrow. His operations were using airfields at Whitchurch close to Bristol and Hurn on the south coast near Bournemouth; the latter, which served transatlantic flights, was regarded as particularly impractical when passengers were obliged to pass Heathrow on their three-hour journeys to and from London.

On 31 May 1944, the government disclosed its plans to the Middlesex County Council, when a compulsory purchase order was drawn up. Using emergency wartime powers, the Air Ministry acquired 2,800 acres, excluding the original Hounslow Heath Customs and military airfield, but including the hamlet Heath Row and the Great West Aerodrome. Fairey Aviation moved to the nearby Heston aerodrome and on 6 June, work began on the runways. Aircraft are required to take off into the prevailing wind, and an RAF triangular pattern of runways was adopted to allow take-offs in any wind direction.

A committee later decided to develop the original pattern into a double-triangle 'Star of David' to permit parallel take-offs and landings. (Heathrow's two major runways today are based on the original north and south sides of the two triangles, Runways 1 and 5.

Following the War, the Labour Government nationalised civil aviation to bring all airports and aerodromes in the UK under the control of the new Ministry of Civil Aviation. This process also included the airlines: three big 'airways corporations' were created: BOAC, serving the Commonwealth, North American and Far Eastern destinations; British South American Airways (BSAA), flying to South America; and British European Airways (BEA), flying UK domestic and short-haul European routes.

Heathrow was still a vast building site on 1 January 1946, when it was transferred from military to civil control and 'Star Light', an Avro Lancastrian of BSAA set off on a historic proving flight to Buenos Aires. Carrying six crew, 10 passengers (a BBC reporter and company officials who would operate the South American end of the service) and a ton of mail, the aircraft flew against strong headwinds and through fog and ice over the Bay of Biscay to Lisbon. After refuelling, it took off for Bathurst in West Africa, where it took on more fuel before leaving on the long haul over the Atlantic. The aircraft arrived at Natal in Brazil in the middle of a tropical rainstorm, and finally reached Buenos Aires over 35 hours after leaving Heathrow. Such was the nature of international travel 70 years ago.

The formal 'London Airport Heath Row' title was adopted from 25 March 1946, by which time BSAA was operating two flights a week. It was joined on the wet blustery morning of 28 May by BOAC when Avro Lancastrian G-AGLS took off on the 'Kangaroo Run' to Sydney. While Lancastrians normally took up to 13 passengers, the need to install bunks on this exceptionally long service, reduced capacity to only six. Each person had an armchair, window and table. International air travel was still very much the domain of the elite.

Below: **Ex-military marquees were used as temporary terminals in 1946. Outside were three telephone boxes, a pillarbox and a mobile post office. The duckboards were laid down so passengers would not sink into the mud as they walked to waiting aircraft.**

Heathrow was opened officially on 31 May 1946 and the first aircraft to land at the new airport was a BOAC Lancastrian from Australia, followed by Lockheed Constellations of Pan American and American Overseas Airways.

The emphasis on construction of the runways rather than terminal capacity led to the creation of a temporary tent village on the north side of the airfield. The early passenger terminals were ex-military marquees which formed a tented village along the Bath Road. The terminals were primitive but comfortable, equipped with floral-patterned armchairs, settees and small tables containing vases of fresh flowers. To reach aircraft parked on the apron, passengers walked over wooden duckboards to protect their footwear from the muddy airfield. There was no heating in the marquees, which meant that during winter it could be bitterly cold, but in summer when the sun shone, the marquee walls were removed to allow a cool breeze to blow through.

Heathrow 1948

Left: Minister of Civil Aviation, Lord Winster (centre at microphone), bids godspeed to passengers and crew travelling on the first official flight to leave London's new airport on 1 January 1946. AVM Donald Bennett, chief executive of British South American Airways and captain of the first flight, an Avro Lancastrian called 'Star Light', is to his left (in uniform).

Below: In 1946 Heathrow was a temporary tent village. The tents were furnished with comfortable chintz armchairs, had a bar, W. H. Smith, a Cable and Wireless Desk and Elsan toilets. Information about arriving and departing flights was chalked on a blackboard.

What's in a name?

An article published in 'Flight magazine' of 19 July 1945, revealed the airport was close to having been called something entirely different from Heathrow. Believing the airport's name might be difficult for foreign crews to pronounce, it had been suggested the airfield should be called Swintonfield, after The Rt Hon Sir Philip Cunliffe-Lister, first Earl of Swinton, who was a Conservative politician (1884-1972) and the UK's first Secretary of State for Air.

For the first 20 years of its operation, it was actually called 'London Airport' before the British Airport Authority renamed it 'Heathrow Airport-London' in 1966.

A row of red telephone boxes and a mobile Post Office stood alongside the tents. Under the canvas the passengers could fortify themselves for the forthcoming 'adventure' in a makeshift bar, browse reading products in a W. H. Smith (the first ever Heathrow retail outlet!), send messages via a Cable & Wireless desk and make use of the Elsan chemical toilets.

Air traffic gradually built up during the first year of operation and a series of ex-military pre-fabricated concrete buildings was soon constructed: 'Warm friendly and bustling, they were in pleasant contrast to the earlier utility accommodation', wrote a BAA historian in the 1960s. By the end of its first year, London Airport had handled approximately 60,000 passengers and 2,400 tons of cargo in around 8,000 movements (take-offs and landings).

Below: A rare colour image of Lancastrian freighter G-AGUL 'Star Watch' of British South American Airways (BSAA), framing an Avro York ZS-ATP 'Springbok'. 'Star Watch' was damaged beyond repair at Heathrow when it ground looped during a night training exercise on 23 October 1947.

Lancastrian interior

The interior of the Lancastrian could be configured with conventional forward-facing seating or with three upper berths with starboard-facing seating underneath.

The wartime ancestry of the Lancastrian is evident in this cockpit view.

Rear freight hold

Toilet

Vestibule & wardrobe

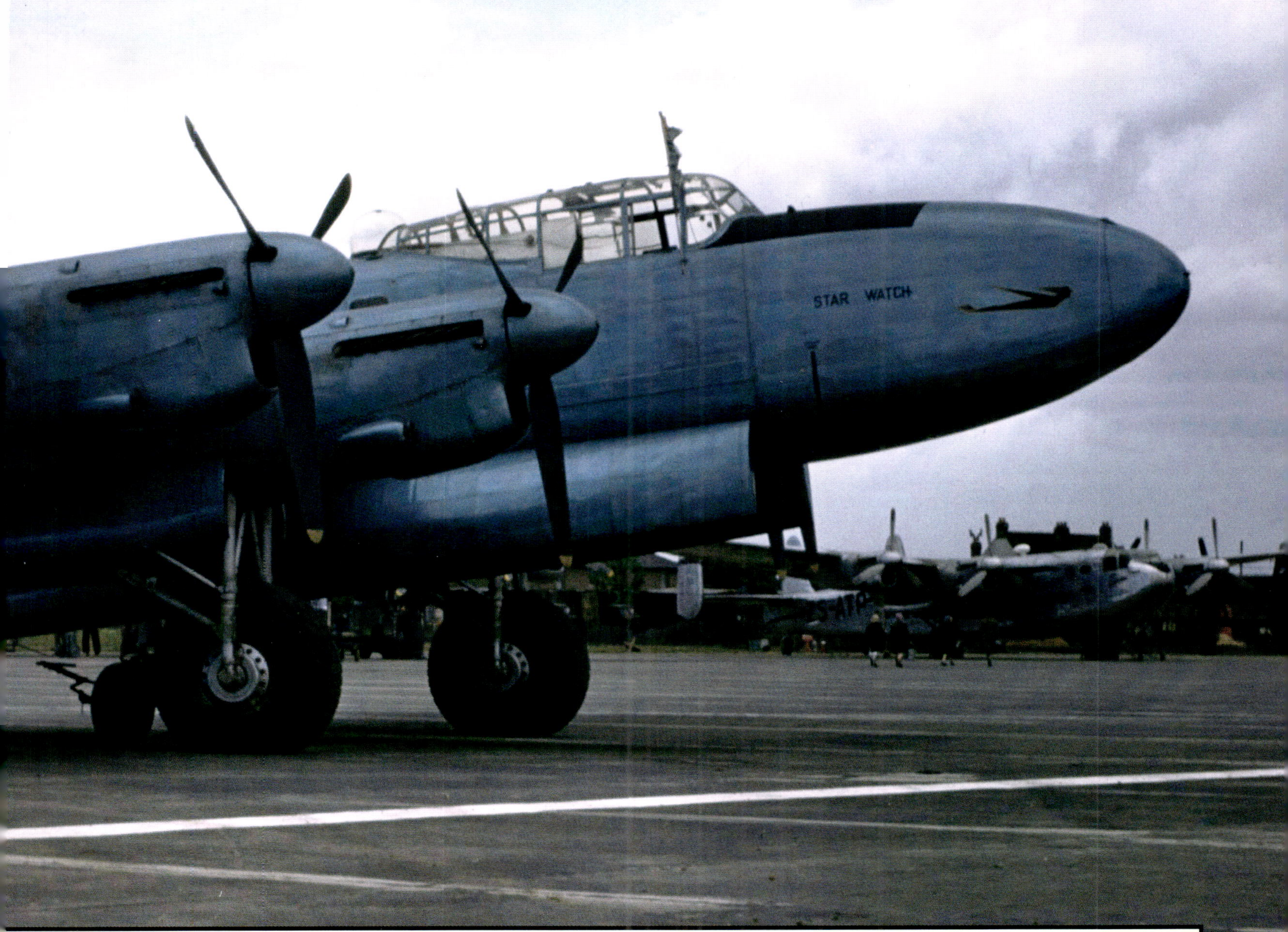

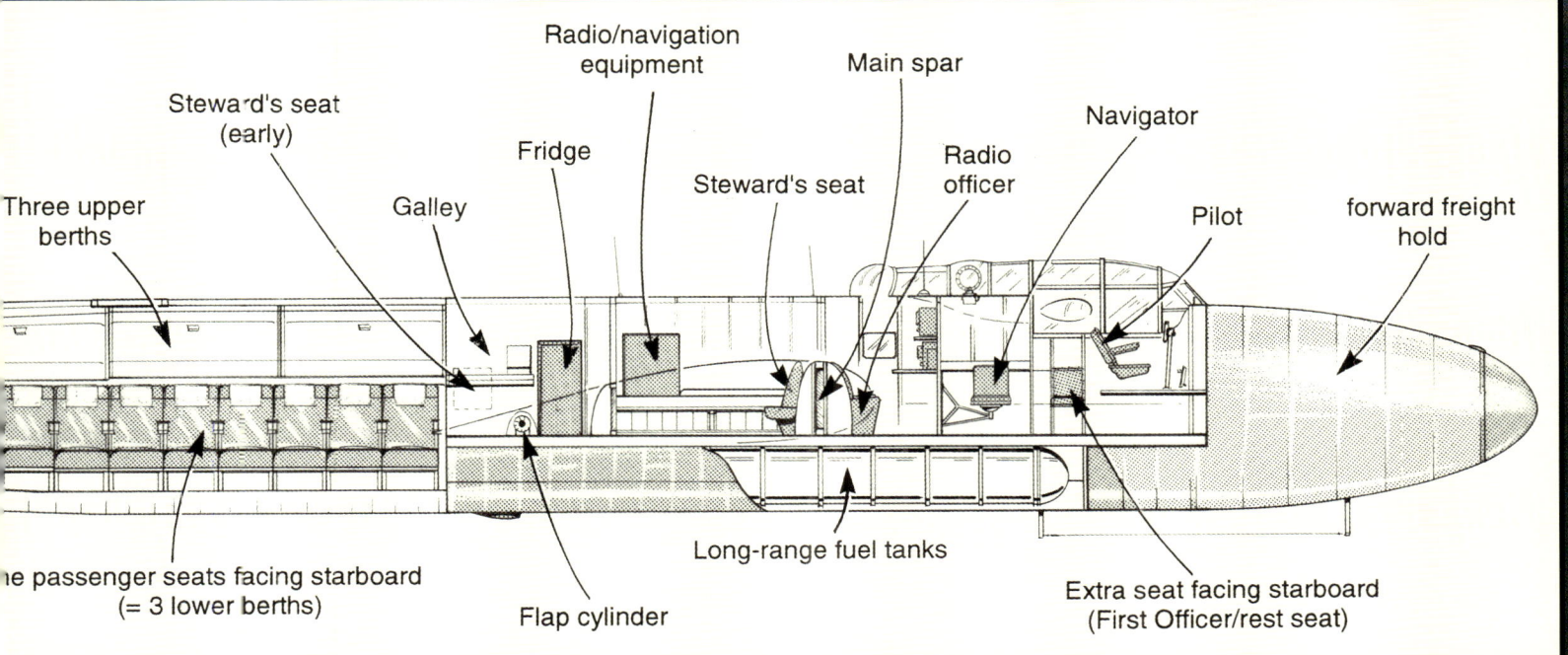

STAR WATCH

Radio/navigation equipment
Main spar
Steward's seat (early)
Navigator
Fridge
Radio officer
Steward's seat
Three upper berths
Galley
Pilot
forward freight hold
Long-range fuel tanks
ne passenger seats facing starboard (= 3 lower berths)
Flap cylinder
Extra seat facing starboard (First Officer/rest seat)

Top and above: **BSAA Avro Tudor IV, 'Star Lion', prepares to board passengers on its inaugural flight from London. The Tudor was a four-engine low-wing monoplane able to carry 32 passengers and a crew of four in its fully-pressurised cabin. Unlike BOAC, which rejected the design, BSAA's Bennett liked the aircraft and stated that it was perfect for his airline. He ordered six enlarged versions of the aircraft, which would be known as the Tudor IV.**

Right: **BSAA Lancastrian 'Star Land' G-AGWI at Heathrow in 1946, with its hinged nose door access to the forward freight hold.**

Top and above: **The airport's first permanent buildings were open by the winter of 1946. Built from postwar prefabricated materials, they were larger more spacious and definitely warmer and more comfortable than the tents they replaced.**

Left: **The race to be the first US airline to land at Heathrow ended in a tie between Constellations operated by Pan American and American Overseas Airways. Although Pan American 'Clipper London' touched down first, both aircraft taxied towards the tented terminal together. Sistership, Pan American N88837 'Clipper Challenge' (pictured), was also a regular visitor to Heathrow in the late 1940s. This aircraft was later converted to L-149 specifications before being sold to Panair do Brasil and registered PP-PDG. Ultimately, on 29 May 1972, it crashed into the jungle in northern Brazil, after all four of its engines had failed.**

A star is born

The Lockheed Constellation played a key role in the early operations of Heathrow airport. As one of the first commercial aircraft designed specifically to operate across the lucrative transatlantic route, Lockheed's graceful airliner blazed the trail, offering passengers unrivalled comfort and speed across the 'pond'. The existence of this most iconic of aircraft can be laid at the door of one man…

In 1939, the top brass of the Lockheed Corporation – president Robert Gross, chief engineer Hall Hibbard, and chief research engineer Kelly Johnson – scheduled a key meeting with a VIP, a man with deep pockets who had recently shown an interest in buying not just one or a handful of new airliners but a fleet of them.

*Above: **All curves and grace, BOAC Lockheed L-049 Constellation G-AHEN 'Baltimore' was delivered on 29 May 1946 and operated many of the early transatlantic flights, as well as flying on routes from Bermuda to Baltimore and New York. When on 5 April 1948 BOAC notched up its 1,000th Constellation-operated North Atlantic crossing, it was with G-AHEN.***

The customer's request had been ambitious. He hoped to hire Lockheed to design a revolutionary aircraft capable of comfortably shuttling 20 passengers and 6,000lb of cargo across the US, offering commercial aviation's first coast-to-coast, non-stop service. But the Lockheed team had even grander ambitions. They were casting their eyes across the Atlantic.

In the years to come, the resulting aircraft would be named the Constellation – Connie

for short – and be flown by airlines around the world, as well as the US military over the ensuing three decades.

But at that moment in 1939 in Los Angeles, the Lockheed Corporation was focused on winning over one customer and one customer only. His name was Howard Hughes.

The Constellation's wing design was close to that of the P-38 Lightning, differing mostly in size. The triple-tail kept the aircraft's height low enough to fit in existing hangars, while other

*Right: **Having left the relative luxury of New York's La Guardia airport, US passengers were somewhat surprised by the less than salubrious surroundings that Heathrow offered in its early years. Here a Trans World Airlines L-749A taxis in at Heathrow after a long flight; note the 'Speedpak' under fuselage freight container.***

features included hydraulically boosted controls and a de-icing system used on wing and tail leading edges. The aircraft had a maximum speed of over 375mph (600km/h), a cruise speed of 340mph (550km/h), and a service ceiling of 24,000ft (7,300m).

After World War Two, the Constellation came into its own as a fast civilian airliner. Aircraft already in production for the USAAF as C-69 transports were finished as civilian airliners, with TWA receiving the first on 1 October 1945. TWA's first transatlantic proving flight departed Washington DC on 3 December 1945, arriving in Paris on 4 December, via Gander and Shannon.

As the first pressurised airliner in widespread use, the Constellation helped to usher in affordable and comfortable air travel, a factor that BOAC was quick to pounce on. On 24 January 1946 it controversially ordered

five L-049 Constellations for transatlantic services, its decision based on the fact that there were no suitable home-grown types available. Thus, on 16 June 1946 Constellation G-AHEM 'Balmoral' operated the first of 10 BOAC transatlantic proving flights and set a record of 11hrs 24min for the New York-London journey, paving the way for the inauguration of twice-weekly scheduled services between London and La Guardia Airport, New York. The Constellations were fitted out in a one-class 43-seat configuration and the services were initially flown via Shannon and Gander.

The stretched Lockheed L-749 variant of the Constellation was the first to regularly cross the Atlantic non-stop, a capability enhanced by its larger fuel capacity, strengthened landing gear and eventually weather radar. Shortly thereafter, the epitome of grace in propeller-

driven aircraft, the 'Super Connie' took to the skies and on 29 September 1957 a TWA L-1649A flew from Los Angeles to London in 18hrs 32min, about 5,420 miles (8,720km) at 292mph (470km/h). The L-1049A still holds the record for the longest-duration, non-stop passenger flight aboard a piston-powered airliner. On TWA's first London-to-San Francisco flight on 1-2 October 1957, the aircraft stayed aloft for 23hrs 19min.

But the Constellation's glory was short lived. The advent of jet airliners such as the de Havilland Comet and Boeing 707, rendered the piston-engined Constellation obsolete. The first routes lost to jets were the long overseas services, the very routes that it had pioneered.

Below: ***A polished metal finish combined with BOAC's speedbird gave Constellation G-AHEK 'Berwick II' a distinctly art deco appeal, a look entirely appropriate for Heathrow's early years.***

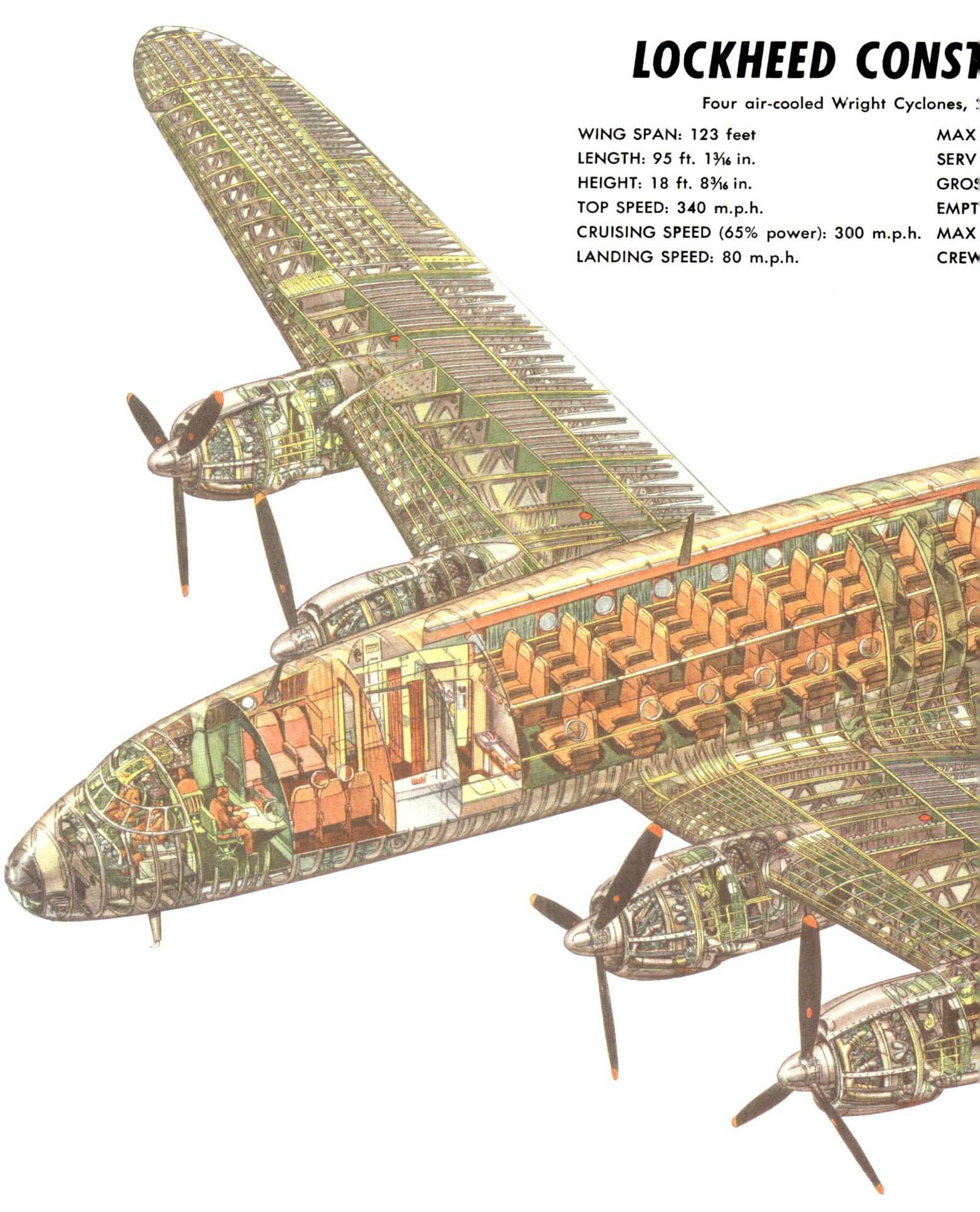

LOCKHEED CONST

Four air-cooled Wright Cyclones, !

WING SPAN: 123 feet
LENGTH: 95 ft. 1³⁄₁₆ in.
HEIGHT: 18 ft. 8³⁄₁₆ in.
TOP SPEED: 340 m.p.h.
CRUISING SPEED (65% power): 300 m.p.h.
LANDING SPEED: 80 m.p.h.

MAX
SERV
GROS
EMPT
MAX
CREW

CRUISER SPEEDBIRD

Relax or have a snack in the comfortable atmosphere of the lower deck lounge.

A spacious cabin so characteristic of the Stratocruiser with convertible sleeping berths.

G–AKGH

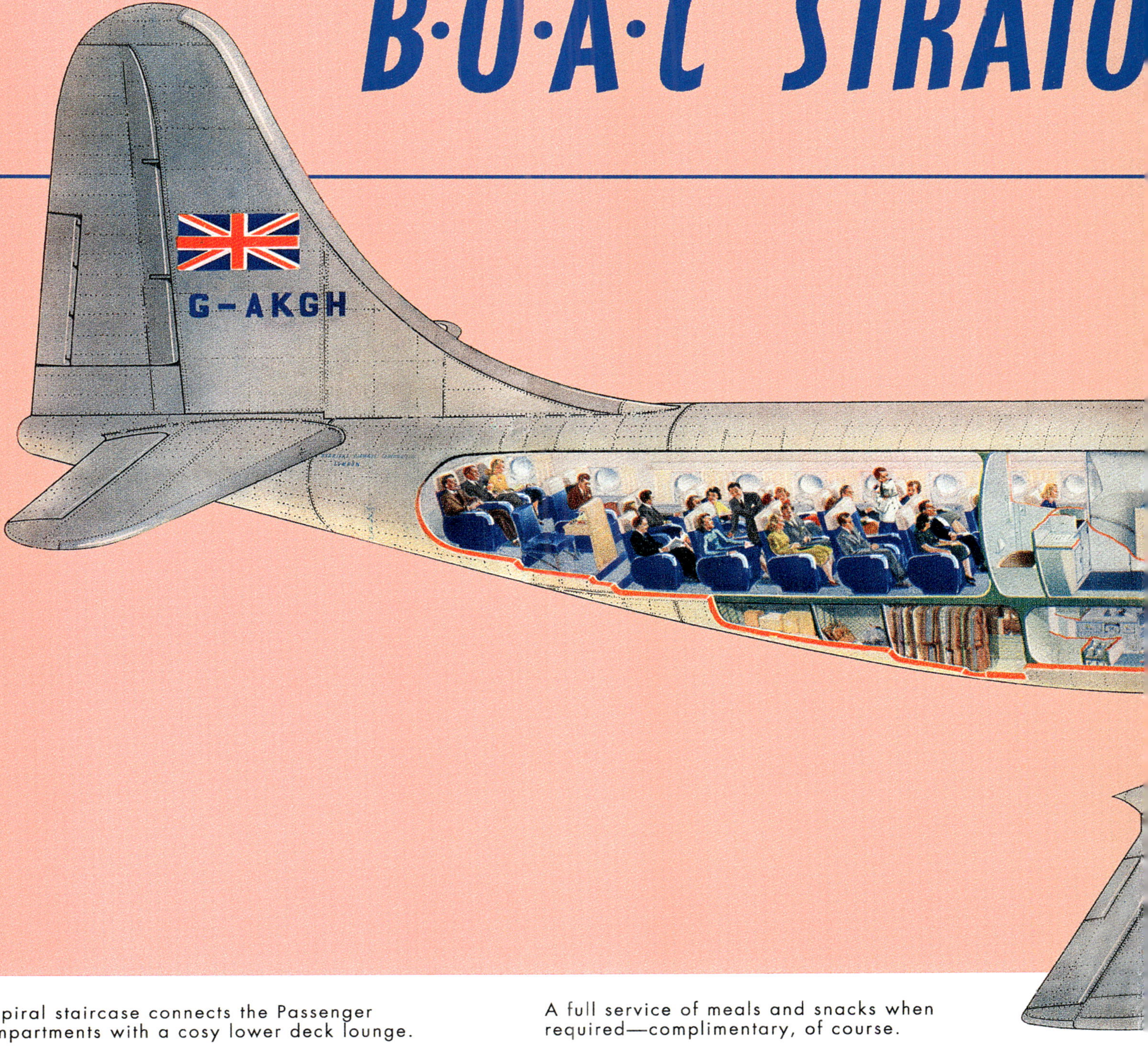

A spiral staircase connects the Passenger compartments with a cosy lower deck lounge.

A full service of meals and snacks when required—complimentary, of course.

ELLATION

,200 h.p. each

MUM RANGE: 4,000 miles

CE CEILING: 25,000 feet

S WEIGHT: 86,250 pounds

Y WEIGHT: 55,550 pounds

MUM PASSENGERS (day): 64

: 6

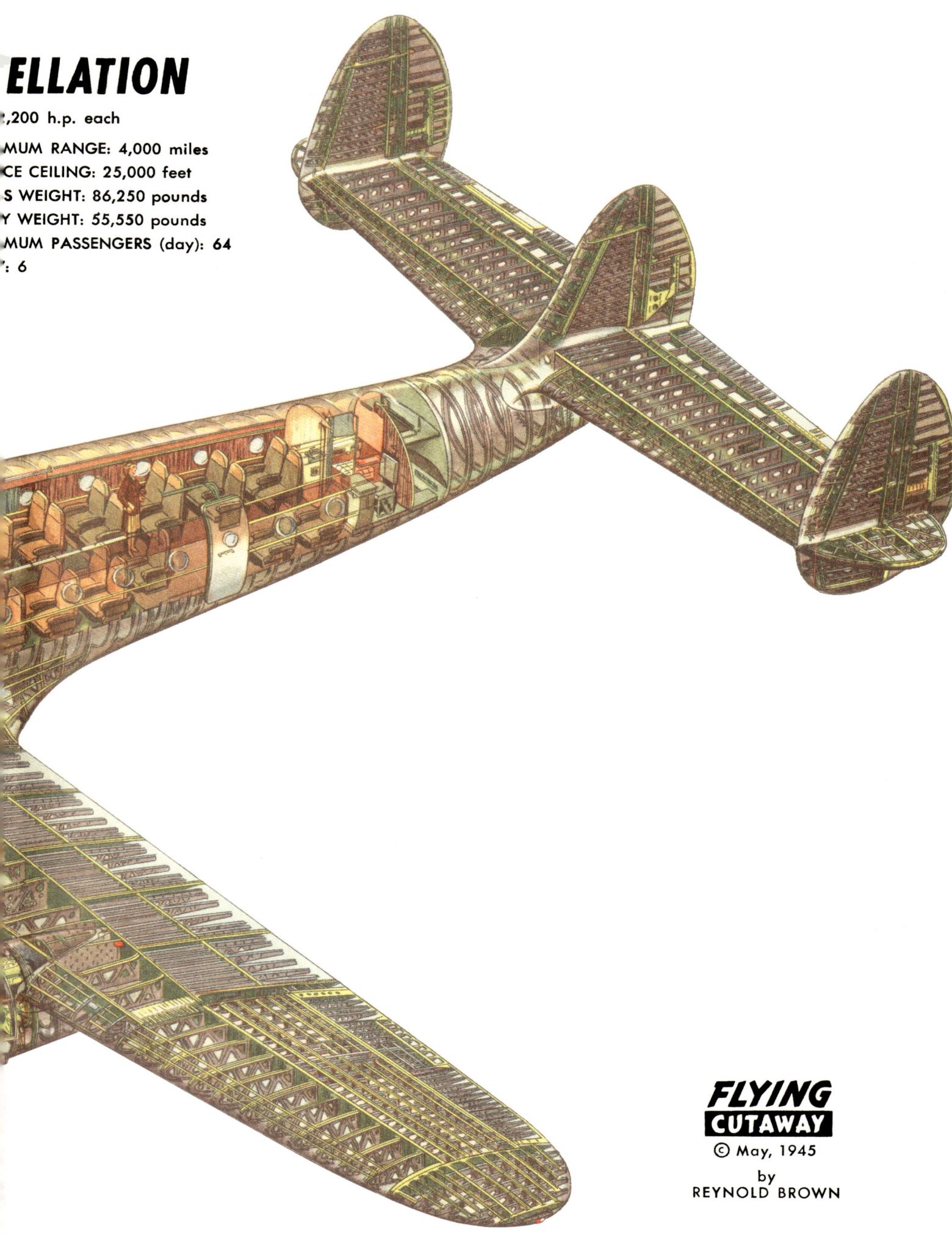

FLYING
CUTAWAY

© May, 1945

by
REYNOLD BROWN

Stratocruiser style

After World War Two, Boeing re-entered the commercial market with a new long-range airliner, the Stratocruiser (Model 377). It was the first Boeing commercial transport since the Stratoliner and was based on the B-29 bomber. Like the rival Constellation, the Stratocruiser played a pivotal role in the early development of Heathrow as a major international gateway.

The prototype Stratocruiser first flew in July 1947, by which time Pan American Airways had already signed a $242 million contract for 20 of the airliners plus spare parts. It was the biggest dollar contract any airline had ever placed up to that time and eventually a total of 55 Stratocruisers was built for use by such customers as BOAC, United Airlines, American Overseas Airlines, SAS and Northwest Airlines. The Model 377 marked Boeing's first significant success selling airliners outside of the US.

Distinguishing features of the Stratocruiser were numerous but the most spectacular of these were concerned with passenger comfort, although performance wise the airliner shaped up pretty well. Powered by four Pratt & Whitney Wasp Major engines, it had a range of approximately 4,400 miles and cruised at a creditable speed of 325mph.

The double-deck interior offered the most luxurious and elegant airborne passenger transport of the time with an upper deck accommodating anything up to 100 passengers (depending on the airline) and featuring sleeping facilities in the form of 28 full-sized Pullman-type berths. Private and semi-private compartments (again, depending on the airline), were provided, together with two dressing rooms and a well-equipped galley. The large flight deck was manned by the pilot, co-pilot and flight engineer, and on

overseas flights a radio operator and navigator also joined the crew. Maximum comfort was ensured by wide aisles between fully adjustable armchair-type seats, the sound-proofed cabin, heating, air conditioning and double-glazed windows. One of the most popular features was the centrally-positioned spiral staircase which led down to the cocktail lounge on the lower deck. The lower deck was divided between the cocktail bar and two large cargo compartments which, on account of their spacious design and folding doors, gave maximum efficiency in cargo handling.

Below: **Flagship of the BOAC Stratocruiser fleet, G-AKGH 'Caledonia' undergoing servicing to its Pratt & Whitney Wasp engines inside the BOAC HQ hangars. Early in its BOAC career, the Stratocruiser suffered from a spate of engine failures, which resulted in a number of aircraft being temporarily grounded while waiting for spares.**

American 'Strats'

Left, right and below: **Launch customer for the Boeing Model 377 Stratocruiser was Pan American World Airways, which wasted no time in putting them onto its transatlantic services, linking New York with London. They were later joined by BOAC as Stratocruisers and Constellations dominated the routes.**

Bottom right: **From Summer 1949, the Constellations of American Overseas Airlines were supplemented and then largely replaced by Boeing Stratocruisers, the first AOA service by the type being on 17 August that year to London Heathrow. AOA was acquired by PAA in 1950 and was merged into what would become Pan American's Atlantic Division. This unit would ultimately become part of Delta Air Lines.**

BOAC took delivery of its first Stratocruiser, G-ALSA 'Cathay', on 15 October 1949 and less than two months later introduced the type on London-New York services, routing via Prestwick, a 19hrs 45min schedule. The De Luxe 'Monarch' service from London to New York was inaugurated on 1 March 1951, with passengers enjoying standards of comfort and service normally only found on ocean liners of the period. These flights entailed a stop at Gander and sometimes Shannon as well.

Meanwhile, Stratocruiser operations through Prestwick were to prove problematic throughout the type's service, as the direction of the main runway was not suited to prevailing winds and the subsidiary runway was not long enough for Stratocruiser operations. Sadly tragedy struck on 25 December 1954 when Stratocruiser G-ALSA 'Cathay' crashed during a landing accident at Prestwick, only eight of the 11 crew and 25 passengers survived.

By early 1955 BOAC's Stratocruiser fleet had increased to 16 machines, with the acquisition of six second-hand examples from United Airlines. Although the airliner continued to offer sterling service, its days of pioneering transatalantic services were coming to an end. BOAC planned to introduce the turboprop Bristol Britannia onto the North Atlantic routes in the mid-1950s but delays in putting the aircraft into service meant that Douglas DC-7s were ordered as a stop gap measure.

In the late 1950s, the 'Strat' was finally withdrawn from regular airline operations, although several were subsequently used by air freight operators – but in 1962 it entered a new and most bizarre role when the first of the grotesque 'Pregnant Guppy' conversions took to the air.

The DOUBLE-DECKED CLIPPER

"STRATO"

- Largest, fastest, most luxurious commercial airliner
- All accommodations finest class
- First ordered, first flown, by Pan American

1 FLIGHT DECK
2 FORWARD COMPARTMENT
3 CLIPPER CARGO
4 MEN'S DRESSING ROOM
   (Ladies' on opposite side)
5 BERTHS
6 SLEEPERETTE
7 LOWER-DECK LOUNGE
8 STAIRWAY TO LOUNGE
9 SERVICE BAR
10 LIFE RAFTS
11 BAGGAGE
12 COAT CLOSET
13 GALLEY

DOUBLE-DECKED "STRATO" CLIPPER DECK PLANS

LOWER DECK LOUNGE
(all Double-Deck "Strato" Clippers)

SLEEPERETTE & BERTH ARRANGEMENT

LOUNGE CHAIR & BERTH ARRANGEMENT

The north side

Although the masterplan for Heathrow had always been to develop the central area at the heart of the runways, early development included expansion of the northern part of the airport that benefitted from easy access from the Bath Road. Indeed, the London Airport North, as it became, was to play an important role in the airport's early growth until its closure in 1961.

From its humble beginnings, the expansion of Heathrow airport was rapid, with postwar prefabricated buildings quickly replacing the 'Tent City'. In keeping with the slightly austere feel to the facilities, a new military-style control tower was erected to direct the ever-increasing flow of air traffic.

Gradually the 'building site' began to evolve into a functional airport with the technology of the day being integrated into the facilities. The operations were still very 'basic' (some would say naive) compared to today's technological

masterpieces, but it worked and gradually the rhythms of a major airport began to be played out. Nevertheless, civil aviation for the masses was still very much in its infancy and the general public was keen to witness the workings of a major airport. Spectators were welcomed and actively encouraged to take bus tours around the airfield, garden parties were organised and the most enthusiastic visitors could even take a pleasure flight over the site for a princely sum of £1 for a 15 min 'spin' in a Rapide! This was not entirely without risk, however, as one Rapide got caught in the wake turbulence of a landing Stratocruiser and crashed within the airfield boundary injuring its occupants. Large viewing areas

Below: ***The north side apron at Heathrow was a very exposed open space that left its aircraft at the mercy of the elements, especially in the depths of winter. Here a pair of snow-capped BEA Viscounts flank an Avro York of Hunting-Clan.***

enclosed by ubiquitous chestnut paling fencing (later metal railings), allowed the public to view these exciting new machines in all their close-up glory, a far cry from the high-security compounds of today.

By 1947, three runways had been completed and work on the other three to form the now-familiar double triangle had begun, although most of these were later used as taxiways. The initial three comprised the main east-west No 1 runway (10L/28R) which was 9,300ft long, to the north side; No 2 Runway (05R/23L) of 6,000ft; and No 6 Runway (33L), also 6,000ft long.

In the 1940s all British airlines except BOAC and BEA operated as charter airlines, flying indigenous types like the Vickers Viking, DH Dove and Avro Anson on short-haul services, plus Lancastrians, Yorks and Tudors for longer haul. Exotic US types like DC-4s, DC-6s, Constellations and Stratocruisers soon ruled the transatlantic routes, but it was not long before the next generation of British turboprop

*Right: **Passengers to London Airport in its early days were greeted by austere functional prefabricated structures rather than buildings of any architectural thought.***

airliners, in the shape of the Viscount and Britannia began to adorn the aprons.

As the newly developed Central Area began to gear up, the northern area was rebranded London Airport North and witnessed the arrival of the first generation of jet airliners. Nevertheless, operations were still very basic with domestic passengers often at the mercy of the elements as they made their way across the wind-swept tarmac to the parked aircraft. Transatlantic passengers were afforded the relative luxury of buses to transport them to and from their waiting mounts.

By the close of Heathrow's first operational year, 63,000 passengers had travelled through London's new airport. By 1951 this had risen to 796,000 and British architect Frederick Gibberd was appointed to design permanent buildings for the airport. Therefore there was a reluctance to sanction the construction of any further buildings on the already inadequate north side area because of the transfer of all passenger handling and air traffic control facilities to the Central Area Site. By 1961 the old terminal on the north side had closed and airlines now either operated from the Europa terminal (later to become Terminal 2) or the Oceanic terminal (eventually Terminal 3).

Left: *Heathrow's original three-story brick RAF-style control tower on the north side of the airfield, together with spectator's enclosure surrounded by chestnut paling fencing, with notice for 'Airport Tours Start Here'.*

Below left: *It might not look like a hot summer's day, but this shot of BOAC Stratocruiser G-ALSD 'Cassiopeia' and BEA Bristol Sycamore helicopter G-ALSR was taken at what was supposed to be the Royal Aeronautical Society Summer Garden Party held at London Airport in 1954.*

Above right: *International travel in the 1950s was largely the domain of the privileged few, such as this chauffeur driven passenger. However a new generation of airliners would soon revolutionise the industry and make flying available for all.*

Far right: *The interior of the international departure lounge was a vast improvement on the tents of a few years earlier.*

Right and below: *DC-4s were regular visitors to Heathrow in the early days, one particularly exotic example being this machine from Air Ceylon VP-CBD 'Laxapana'.*

SYE 314

VP-C
K·L·M

AIR-INDIA
KLM ROYAL DUTCH AIRLINES
INSURANCE
INSURANCE
CONCOURSE BUFFET

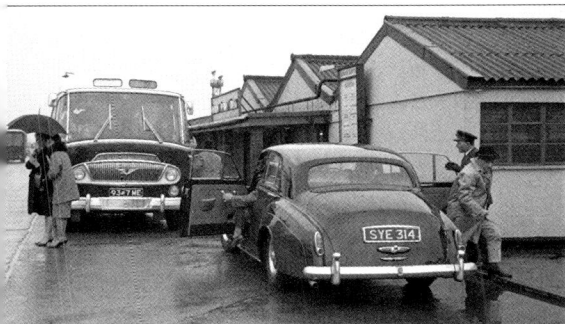

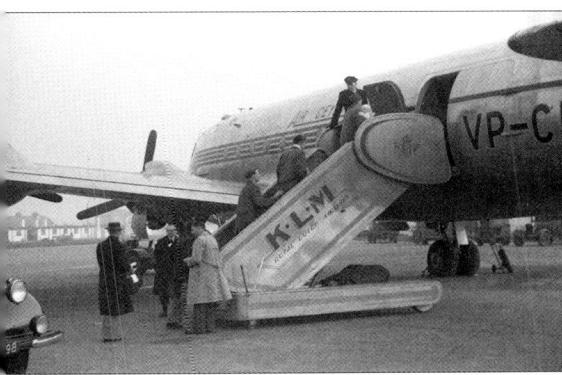

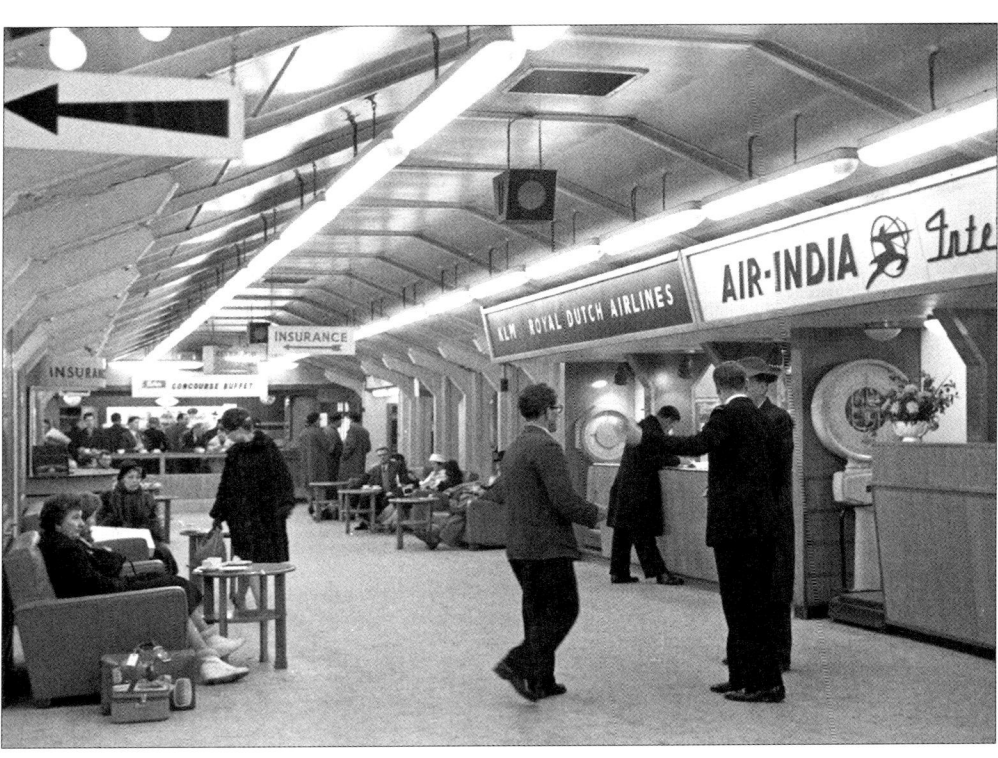

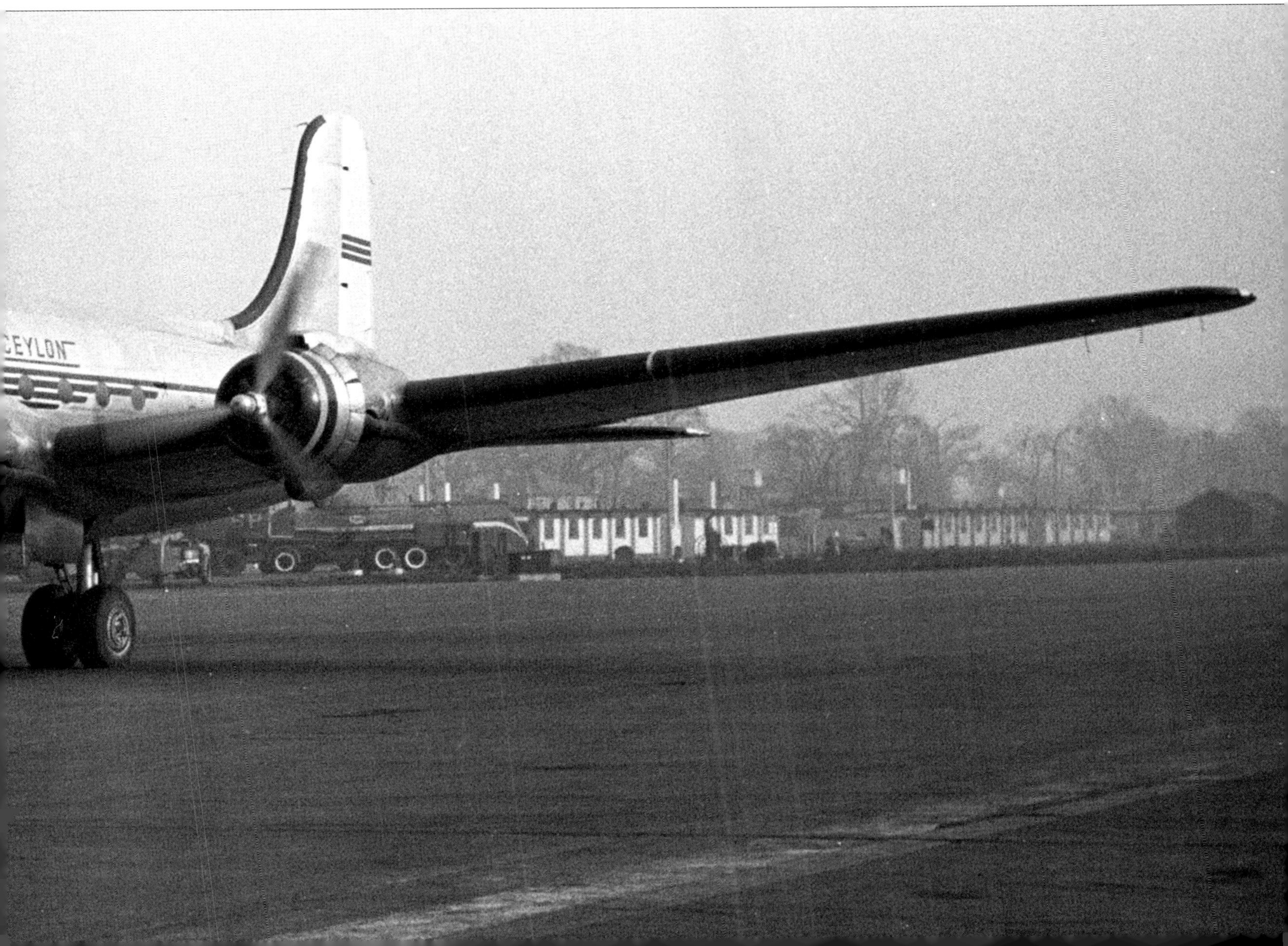
CEYLON

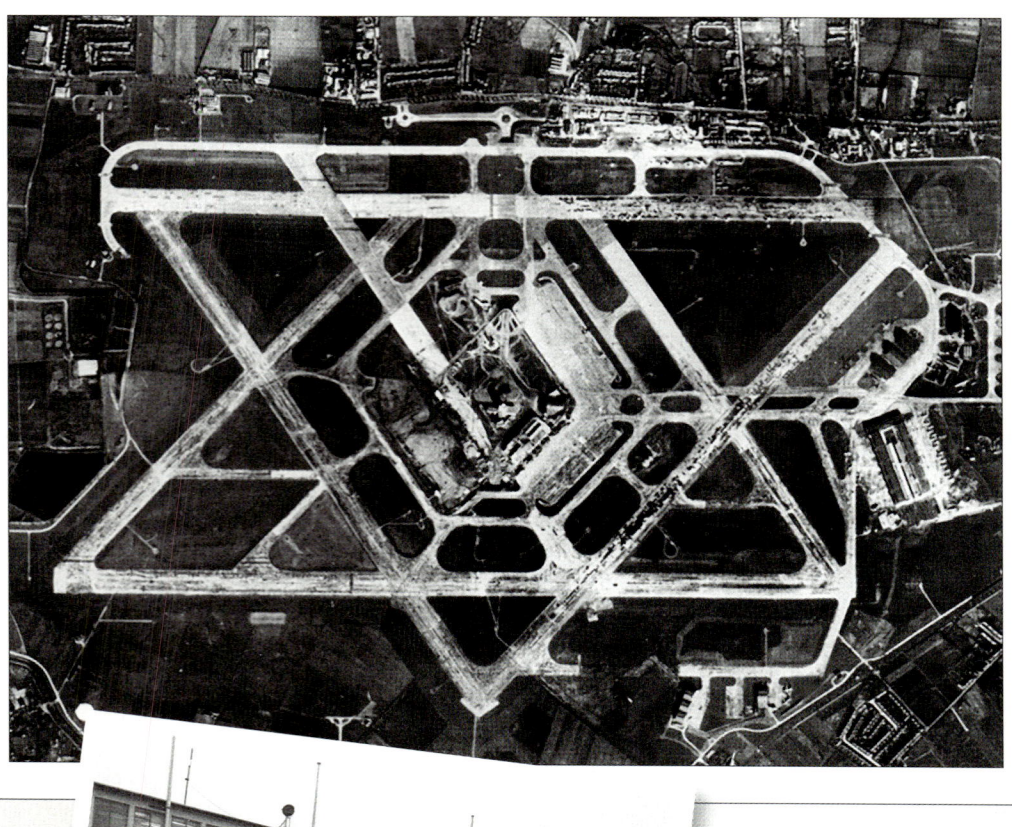

Left: The Heathrow layout in 1955 began to take on a very familiar appearance with work progressing on the central area, engineering buildings and hangars to the eastern end and business still focussed on the London Airport North, alongside the Bath Road (top).

Inset left: Passengers brave the elements as they leave the departure lounge of London Airport and make their way across the apron towards their aircraft.

Right: A shot that epitomises Heathrow in the late 1950s and encompasses three generations of airliners. Heading the line is piston power in the shape of the Skyways of London Avro York G-ANVO, while Bristol Britannia G-ANBH of BOAC boasted the thrust of turboprops. Finally, the all-conquering jet airliner is represented by a newly-delivered Boeing 707 of Pan American operating one of its first transatlantic flights.

Below: Before the central area was open for business, the north side played host to the new generation of airliners, including this Pan Am Boeing 707, KLM Viscount and BOAC 707s, all casting their reflections on yet another damp London day .

Propliner parade

Above: **The glory of another age, with props as far as the eye can see on a cold wintry day at Heathrow's Central Area. Heading the line is sleek BOAC Britannia 312 G-AOVF, framing the shape of one of the carrier's DC-7C propliners, G-AOID, ordered as a stopgap because of the late delivery of the Bristol design. A KLM De Vliegende Hollander (Flying Dutchman) L-749A Constellation PH-LDE heads a pair of Viscounts of BOAC associate BWIA – British West Indian Airways – and beyond that are DC-7s of various US carriers that plied their trade on the transatlantic routes.**

For many years Heathrow echoed to the throbbing soundtrack of pistons and turboprops. Some of the world's most charismatic and iconic propliners were to be seen across the open concrete expanses of the new airport.

It was still a time of wonderment, a time when flying was viewed as an exotic adventure for the privileged few. It was also a time when no two airliner designs looked alike, this hand-crafted individualism giving them charm and, most of all, personality. While the aforementioned Constellations and Stratocruisers might have dominated the aprons in the early years, here we present a small selection of some other exotic, rare and unusual beasts. Sit back and enjoy Heathrow at its finest.

Above: **Possibly not the most conventional of ways for a pilot to enter his aircraft. BSAA Avro Tudor IV 'Star Lion' is readied for its first services from London, while a DC-3 looks on from the distance. Although BOAC and other foreign airlines agreed to purchase some American aircraft, AVM Bennett of BSAA bought the British-built Tudor for his fleet.**

Left: **Daily life at London Airport as a Hunting Clan Vickers Viking is refuelled from a Shell fuel tanker.**

Below: **An Airspeed Ambassador kicks into life in front of the immense BEA engineering base at Heathrow. Dubbed the Elizabethan by the carrier, it operated the pride of BEA's early routes, the daily 'Silver Wing' London-Paris service. BEA's publicity material at the time waxed lyrical about the aircraft: 'So quiet you can talk in whispers. Steady in flight, watch the cocktail in your glass stay level. Air conditioned, an atmosphere of luxury. Superbly comfortable armchairs… the Airspeed Elizabethan makes air travel a greater pleasure than ever before.'**

G-AGPW

Above and left: Brabazon, the world's largest airliner at the time and the shining hope of British aviation, made its one and only visit to Heathrow in mid June 1950. Spectators flocked to see the gleaming mighty beast that dwarfed everything else at the airport, including Stratocruisers. But the 'elitist' concept of the aircraft was misguided and the project was doomed to fail even before it had got air under its tyres. The Brabazon made three take-offs and landings at Heathrow, before lumbering off into the distance never to be seen at the airport again.

Left: **Room with a view, or more precisely, restaurant with a view. While you tuck into your traditional breakfast, you could be entertained by the workings of an international airport, provided here by a visiting Alitalia DC-6B, I-DIMD, sharing the apron with resident BEA Viscount. In the background is the former Fairey hangar, now sporting a BOAC advertising hoarding.**

Right: **Inside the vast BEA engineering complex, Vickers Viscount G-AMOB comes in for some regular maintenance. Delivered to BEA on 24 April 1953 'Oscar Bravo' was named 'R M A William Baffin' and was fitted with Rolls-Royce Dart RDa3 Mark 505 engines. Later it was to operate the first Viscount services to both Valencia and Warsaw, before it was sold to Brazilian carrier VASP in 1962 for £110,000. It was finally withdrawn from service in 1975 and scrapped four years later.**

Below right: **The elegant lines of the Lockheed Electra gracing the apron of London Airport North on 17 May 1960. KLM was the only European airline to order the type from Lockheed and operated 12 between September 1959 and January 1969 in Europe and east to Saigon and Kuala Lumpur.**

Below: **A delightful study of an Air Ceylon Douglas DC-4 during turnaround at Heathrow, before departing for its long haul down to Australia. Even by 1950 standards, this baggage truck looks distinctly old-fashioned!**

S 310
Proteus 755 Turboprops

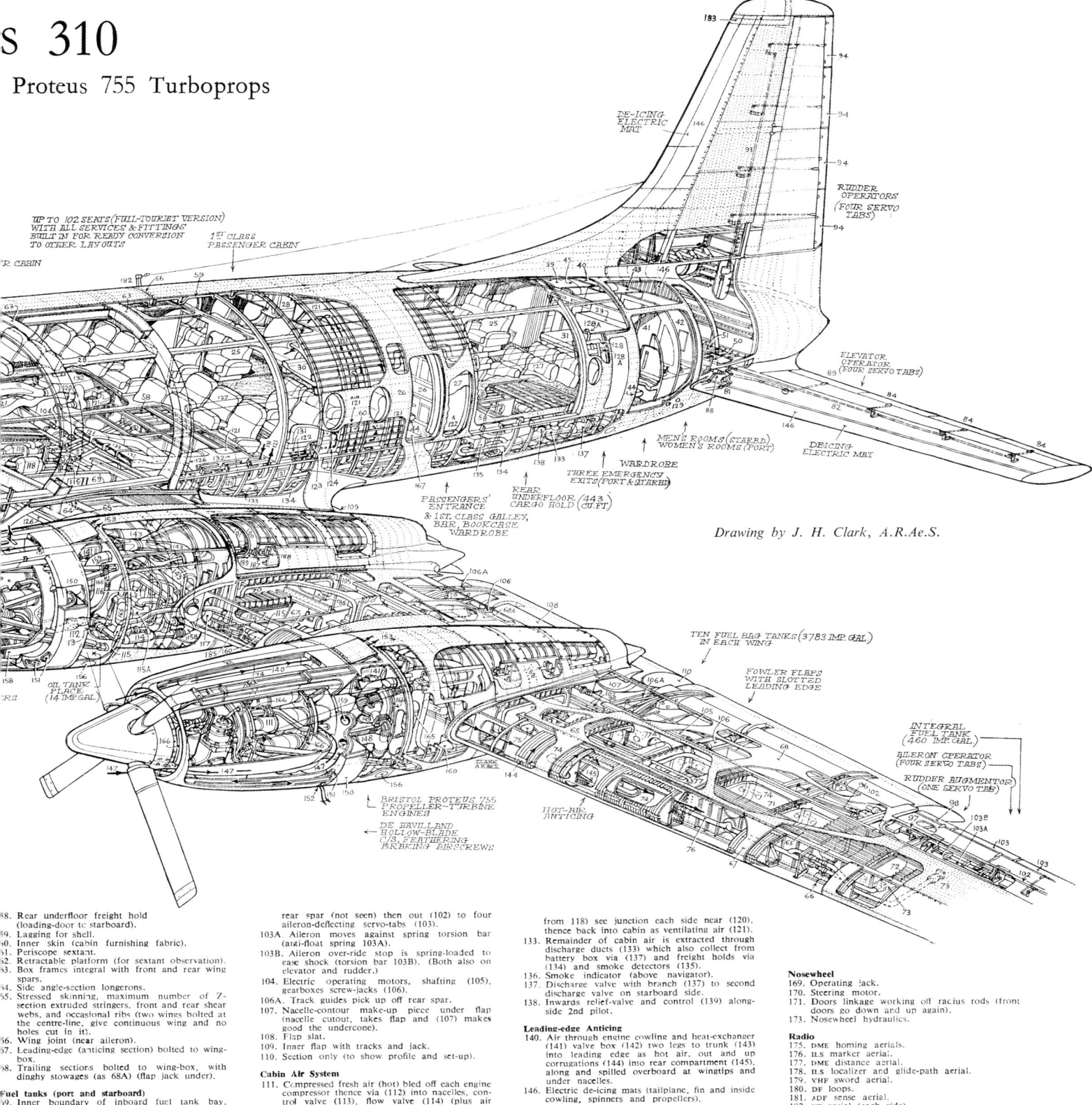

UP TO 102 SEATS (FULL-TOURIST VERSION)
WITH ALL SERVICES & FITTINGS
BUILT IN FOR READY CONVERSION
TO OTHER LAYOUTS

1ST CLASS PASSENGER CABIN

DE-ICING ELECTRIC MAT

RUDDER OPERATORS (FOUR SERVO TABS)

ELEVATOR OPERATOR (FOUR SERVO TABS)

DE-ICING ELECTRIC MAT

MEN'S ROOMS (STARB'D) WOMEN'S ROOMS (PORT)

WARDROBE

THREE EMERGENCY EXITS (PORT & STARB'D)

REAR UNDERFLOOR CARGO HOLD (443 CU.FT)

PASSENGERS' ENTRANCE & 1ST CLASS GALLEY, BAR, BOOKCASE, WARDROBE

Drawing by J. H. Clark, A.R.Ae.S.

OIL TANK PLACE (14 IMP GAL)

TEN FUEL BAG TANKS (3783 IMP. GAL) IN EACH WING

FOWLER FLAPS WITH SLOTTED LEADING EDGE

INTEGRAL FUEL TANK (460 IMP. GAL)

AILERON OPERATOR (FOUR SERVO TABS)

RUDDER AUGMENTOR (ONE SERVO TAB)

HOT-AIR ANTICING

BRISTOL PROTEUS 755 PROPELLER-TURBINE ENGINES

DE HAVILLAND HOLLOW-BLADE C/S FEATHERING BRAKING AIRSCREWS

---

58. Rear underfloor freight hold (loading-door to starboard).
59. Lagging for shell.
60. Inner skin (cabin furnishing fabric).
61. Periscope sextant.
62. Retractable platform (for sextant observation).
63. Box frames integral with front and rear wing spars.
64. Side angle-section longerons.
65. Stressed skinning, maximum number of Z-section extruded stringers, front and rear shear webs, and occasional ribs (two wings bolted at the centre-line, give continuous wing and no holes cut in it).
66. Wing joint (near aileron).
67. Leading-edge (anticing section) bolted to wing-box.
68. Trailing sections bolted to wing-box, with dinghy stowages (as 68A) (flap jack under).

Fuel tanks (port and starboard)
69. Inner boundary of inboard fuel tank bay, which extends to centre-line rib of inboard nacelle (70) middle bay extends to centre-line of outboard nacelle (70) beyond which is outer bay (71).
72. Integral tank out to wing tip (front rib 72).
73. Fuel pumps.
74. Balance pipes.
75. Emergency fillers (three in all) along each wing.
76. Charging pipe from pressure refuelling point at rear under outboard nacelle.
77. Vent pipe.
77A. Manhole to bag tanks.

Flying Controls
78. Push-pull stick to control unit (79) and autopilot servo motor, thence via underfloor trough in freight holds (80) to screw jacks (81)—shown displaced—against tailplane rear spar and rods (82) to three servo-tabs (84).
85. Trim wheel in cockpit console (9) down to autopilot trim motor (86), along underfloor trough (87), to bevel box (88) at tailplane spar end tab (89).
90. Rudder pedals to control unit (91) and autopilot servo motor underfloor trough (92), vertical shaft up rudder post (93) to four operating tabs (94).
95. At wing rear spar a gearbox branch-off runs out via rods (96) and (97) to aileron inboard tab (98).
99. From control wheel (99) to control unit (100), underfloor trough (101) to bevel box at wing

rear spar (not seen) then out (102) to four aileron-deflecting servo-tabs (103).
103A. Aileron moves against spring torsion bar (anti-float spring 103A).
103B. Aileron over-ride stop is spring-loaded to ease shock (torsion bar 103B). (Both also on elevator and rudder.)
104. Electric operating motors, shafting (105), gearboxes screw-jacks (106).
106A. Track guides pick up off rear spar.
107. Nacelle-contour make-up piece under flap (nacelle cutout, takes flap and (107) makes good the undercone).
108. Flap slat.
109. Inner flap with tracks and jack.
110. Section only (to show profile and set-up).

Cabin Air System
111. Compressed fresh air (hot) bled off each engine compressor thence via (112) into nacelles, control valve (113), flow valve (114) (plus air (115) from outboard engines), temp.-control valve (115B), and either through cooler (115A) and cold-air unit (116) or direct (117) to water separators (118) and to dumping valves (119), thence through humidifier and jet pump (120), into trunk (121).
121. Ventilating-air trunks feed air up between some frames (each side) up between skin and inner skin (60) to ceiling space (28) thence through porous cloth furnishing into cabin.
121A. Ceiling extension for cockpit.
122. Fresh conditioned-air tapping off (118) (see wingspars in fuselage) feeds continuous floor trunk (123) (see wing root trailing edge) which feeds air (124) into double skin, up and out into cabin under the windows (and above baggage rack in bays except those carrying air 121).
122A. Balance pipe for air (122).
125. Branches of (122) supply air to freight holds and control units, controls and cockpit.
126. Cold-air tapping off cold-air unit feeds passengers individual-control louvres above windows via trunk (127).
127. Supplies air to trunk (128) behind bunk with extensions (128A) up and down to seat and bunk louvres (sleeper version).
129. Air extractors from galleys and lavatories.
130. Some air is drawn out of cabin through large-area vents and filters (130) and floor-sinks (131) into and along trunks (132) to the point where it mixes with new incoming air (trunk

from 118) see junction each side near (120), thence back into cabin as ventilating air (121).
133. Remainder of cabin air is extracted through discharge ducts (133) which also collect from battery box via (137) and freight holds via (134) and smoke detectors (135).
136. Smoke indicator (above navigator).
137. Discharge valve with branch (137) to second discharge valve on starboard side.
138. Inwards relief-valve and control (139) alongside 2nd pilot.

Leading-edge Anticing
140. Air through engine cowling and heat-exchanger (141) valve box (142) two legs to trunk (143) into leading edge as hot air, out and up corrugations (144) into rear compartment (145), along and spilled overboard at wingtips and under nacelles.
146. Electric de-icing mats (tailplane, fin and inside cowling, spinners and propellers).

Engine Cowling Anticing and Air Systems
147. Engine compressor supply.
148. Bleed mixes with hot gas (149) (gas-turbine bleed—actually on starboard side) to provide anticing air into and around annulus (150) then out via (151) into and along cowling, back and spill to atmosphere at (152).
149. Turbine gas also passes up through heat exchanger (141) and out at spill valve (153).
154. Air scoops for cooling air to generator (155), outlet (156) using some of main air (147).
157. Wall around generator makes "island" in the airflow (147).
158. Oil cooler takes some air (147).
159. Bleed (each side of nacelle) air to cooler (115A) and transformer/rectifiers (160).
160. Power-egg front hoist points.

Engine Fire Protection
161. No. 1 fire zone.
162. No. 2 fire zone.
163. No. 2A fire zone (oil tank is in zone 2A).
164. No. 3 fireproof zone (nacelle).
165. Three bottles per nacelle.
166. Spray rings.

Fuselage Fire Protection
167. Floor-hatch access to bottles in underfloor and one (over) for electrical bay, bottles feed sprays (168) on vertical supports (into freight holds) and to wing roots.
168. Bottle (above navigator).

Nosewheel
169. Operating jack.
170. Steering motor.
171. Doors linkage working off radius rods (front doors go down and up again).
173. Nosewheel hydraulics.

Radio
175. DME homing aerials.
176. ILS marker aerial.
177. DME distance aerial.
178. ILS localizer and glide-path aerial.
179. VHF sword aerial.
180. DF loops.
181. ADF sense aerial.
182. HF aerial (each side).
183. MF/HF reception suppressed aerial and spark gap (top of fin).

Main Undercarriage and Nacelle
184. Two undersurface beams with radius-rod pick up (185).
186. Main-undercarriage pick up on rear shear web.
187. Beam supported by (188).
189. Rollers carry heat shroud (190) in beam (187).
191. Jet tube in (190).

UPSWEPT WING-TIP

JET EFFLUX

TOURIST PASSENG

NAVIGATOR
SUPERNUMERARY
RADIO OP.

FIRST OFFICER

CAPTAIN

DROP-AWAY NOSE GOOD OUTLOOK

RADAR

STEERING NOSEWHEEL IN UNPRESSURIZED BAY

CREW'S ENTRANCE

MAIL COMPT. (PORT)

FORWARD UNDERFLOOR CARGO-HOLD (386 CU FT)

CREW'S ROOMS (PORT & STARB'D)
BAGGAGE (PORT)

GALLEY & CREW'S RESTROOM (STARB'D)

ELECTRIC ANTICING AIRSCREWS & SPINN

The AEROPLANE COPYRIGHT

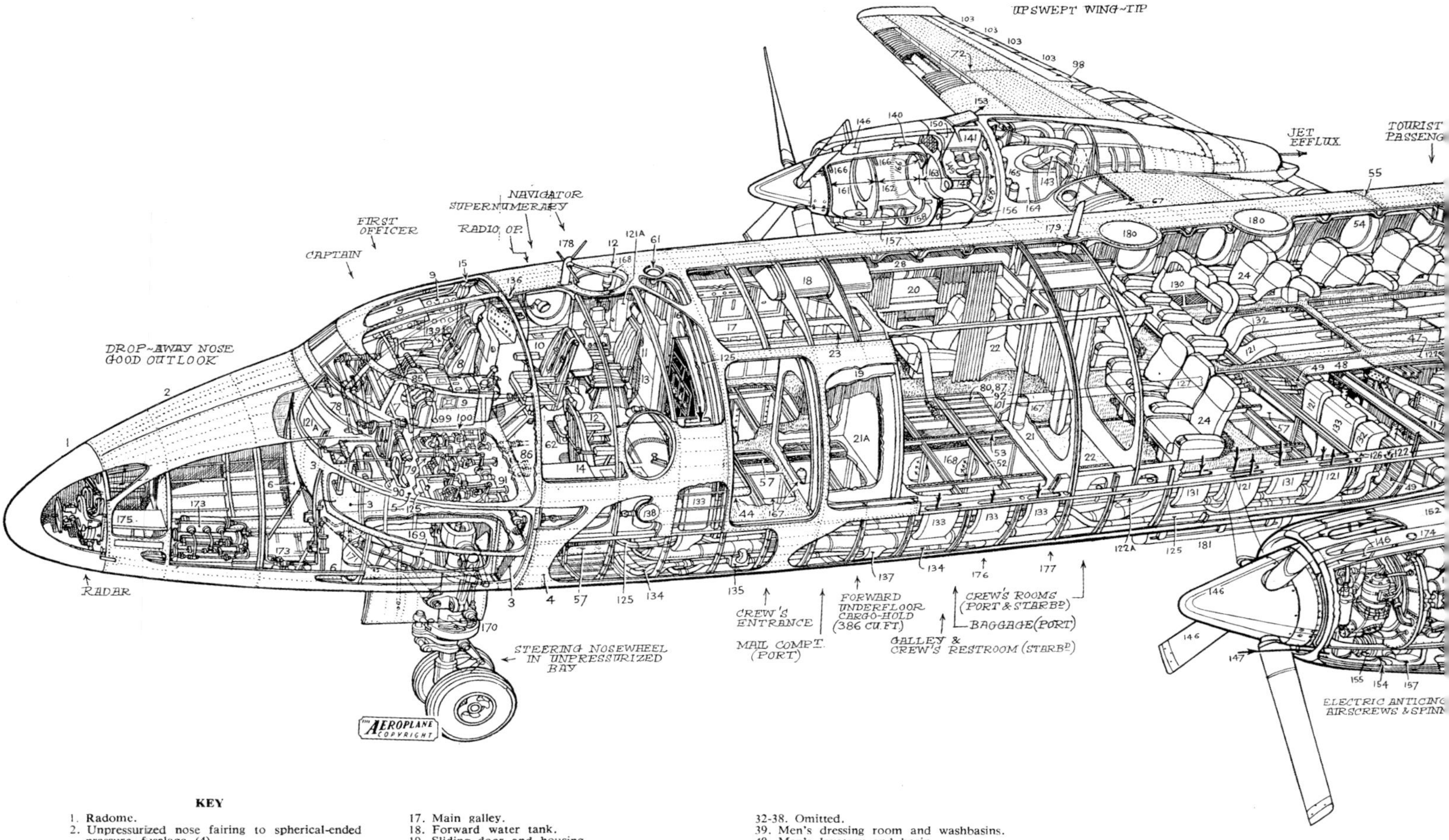

KEY

1. Radome.
2. Unpressurized nose fairing to spherical-ended pressure fuselage (4).
3. Spherical-ended flat-bottomed and vertical bulkheads (pressure-end).
5. Upper pilots' floor.
6. Horn-plates carrying nosewheel.
7. Windscreen with heating and direct-vision panel (7).
8. 1st and 2nd pilots' seats.
9. Roof and side panels and centre console.
10. Supernumerary's place (two-height).
11. Navigator's station.
12. Ditching hatch.
13. Fuse box and electrics panels.
14. Radio operator's position.
15. Night curtains.
16. Door (with self-contained service hatch from galley).

17. Main galley.
18. Forward water tank.
19. Sliding door and housing.
20. Crew's rest room (2 bunks, 2 seats).
21. Baggage compartment (port).
21A. Diplomatic mail or additional baggage.
22. Crew's lavatory and washroom (each side).
23. Door (with service hatch from galley).
24. Main passenger cabin (tourist section).
25. Main passenger cabin (1st class, one arrangement of several).
26. Pantry, cocktail bar, coats or bookcase.
27. Sliding passenger-door and housing.
28. Line of ceiling (with ceiling-lighting and air supply).
29. Coats and end (emergency) door each side.
30. Light luggage rack.
31. Line of (alternatively) bunks.

32-38. Omitted.
39. Men's dressing room and washbasins.
40. Men's lavatory and basin.
41. Women's dressing room, dressing table and basins.
42. Women's room and basin.
43. 3rd lavatory (quick change-over men/women as required according to immediate flight passenger list).
44. Steward's landing seat—in (41) and see also at doors (27) and (19).
45. Line of rear water tanks above ceiling.
46. Rear pressure bulkhead.
47. The rear spar of wing, the top surface of wing (with horizontal extension plate (48) and vertical bulkhead (49)) together with fuselage-shell (4) and items (3) and (46) make up pressure shell.

50. Tailplane box (just seen, and sectioned to lay bare controls (81), etc., just behind it) with decking (51) over.
52. Fuselage floor cutaways reveal continuous cross-members with intercostal fore-and-aft members carrying seat-rails (53) designed for all types of seating (International Standard).
54. Deep elliptical double-glazed anti-misting windows (with several of emergency-exit type along each side).
55 to 56. Centre-section between joints (55) and (56) bolted-up to wing (front and rear fuselages then added).
57. Forward underfloor freight hold (loading-door to starboard).

Left: **Britannias in the mist, outside the huge hangars of the BOAC engineering base. By the time the Britannia's troubled development was completed, 'pure' jet airliners were about to enter service and consequently only 85 were built before production ended in 1960. Nevertheless, the Britannia is considered one of the landmarks in turboprop-powered airliner design and was popular with passengers. It became known by the title of 'The Whispering Giant' for its quiet exterior noise and smooth flying.**

Right: **Sir Reginald Verdon-Smith, right, head of Bristol Aeroplane Company, hands over the first Bristol Britannia 100 to Sir Miles Thomas, chairman of BOAC at London Airport on 30 December 1955, ready for crew training. The Model 102 began scheduled service on 1 February 1957 with a BOAC flight from London to Johannesburg, with flights to Sydney following in March and to Tokyo in July. By August 1957, the first 15 Model 102 aircraft had been delivered to BOAC.**

Central area

World War Two had postponed the natural growth of civil aviation in the UK by six years, and uncertainty over future demand made planning Heathrow's future difficult. But as more accurate forecasts became available, a master plan was developed for terminals and an air-traffic control tower on a central site linked with the A4 Bath Road by twin road tunnels.

Frederick Gibberd was appointed architect, and construction began in 1951. BOAC, which had absorbed BSAA, continued to operate its long-haul routes from the north side area, while BEA served domestic and European destinations from nearby Northolt, loaned from the RAF during Heathrow's development. On 31 October 1954, Northolt reverted to military use, and BEA and other European operators moved to Heathrow.

Heathrow's first terminal, the 'Europa Building' (later Terminal 2), opened for short-haul flights on 17 April 1955; an annex called the 'Britannic' was used for BEA's domestic and European routes, and facilities for pilots debriefing, administrative offices, restaurants and a spectators' viewing area were provided in the adjacent 'Queen's Building'. The London Air Traffic Control Centre transferred from Uxbridge to the newly completed tower, and all three Central Terminal Area buildings were inaugurated by Her Majesty the Queen on 16 December, 1955.

The airport continued to grow and in mid-1957 the Milbourn Committee – established to plan its future expansion – proposed construction of a long-haul terminal, a second

short-haul building and a cargo terminal in the southwest corner of the airport.

Long-haul flights operated from the original North Side facilities until 16 November 1961 when BOAC transferred to the new 'Oceanic Building' (later Terminal 3), followed on 28 March 1962, by remaining long-haul airlines.

By the mid-1960s, the bureaucracy associated with Government management of Britain's airports, particularly Heathrow, was considered inappropriate and in 1966 the British Airports Authority (BAA) was established to run London's Heathrow, Gatwick and Stansted, and Prestwick Airport near Glasgow. In 1968, BAA plc was created, but remained government-owned until privatisation took place in 1987. During the mid/late-1960s, Heathrow became the site of a £130 million capital-investment programme as the other recommendations of the Milbourn Committee took effect. The new short-haul building (later Terminal 1) came into operation in 1968 for UK airline services, which had previously operated from the 'Britannic' annex. Formally opened by Her Majesty The Queen on 17 April, the following year, Terminal 1 the largest airport terminal in Europe, set the standard for 'a new era in air travel'.

The cargo part of the plan was also coming to fruition with the development of a 160-acre site

and a tunnel to link it to the Central Terminal Area. The new centre opened in 1968.

And in 1970, the capital investment continued with the arrival of the Boeing 747 jumbo jet which necessitated an expansion of Terminal 3. The original building was used solely for departures, and a completely new arrivals area was added. A special new complex of pier, gate-room and air-jetty systems was installed, moving walkways were introduced to reach them (the first in the UK), and the airport's runways were also extended to approximately 2.5 miles. Heathrow was now leading the way in airport technology.

*Left: **Packed crowds look on as a BEA Comet 4B taxies past a pair of Viscounts and the central terminal buildings at London Airport. This was a time when spectators were still actively encouraged to watch proceedings, indeed Heathrow became a top tourist attraction.***

*Top right: **By the 1960s visitors arriving through Heathrow's new access tunnel were greeted with a 'new look' that befitted the airport's growing role as a gateway to the world. Its distinctive control tower was to remain a significant landmark for many years.***

*Right: **Inside, the new central airport terminal was spacious and well lit, in stark contrast to the previous building on the north side.***

Left: Inside the all-seeing control tower during its early operation. On the surface all appears to be calm!

Right: Long-haul passengers view some of BOAC's fleet of Boeing 707s from the terminal balcony on 24 December 1961.

Below: The Central Area still underdevelopment in the late1960s, but now with the Queen's building (centre) flanked by the newly completed Terminal 1 to the left and Terminal 2 (the old Passenger Building), to the right, behind the control tower.

Above: **Suitably wrapped up well in typical 1960's fashion, a family waves off passengers boarding a BEA Vanguard.**

Right: **Swinging sixties. The departure hall in the original Europa terminal in 1965 reflected the chic fashions of the era.**

Below **The approach to the new Terminal 1, that was opened in 1968 and became the home of all BEA's pan-European services. The original Europa terminal would now be renamed Terminal 2 and be used by continental European airlines, while the Oceanic Building operating long-haul flights would be renamed Terminal 3.**

Above left: **Terminal 3 became the hub for long-haul international flights, which could explain the brash presence of the Ford Starliner sitting outside!**

Above right: **Heathrow baggage carousel in the new Terminal 1.**

Left: **Tridents galore, as viewed from the roof gardens of Heathrow's Central Area. When the gardens were first opened in 1955, they became Britain's top visitor attraction and people dressed up for the occasion, a tradition that appears to have continued into the 1960s, judging from this image.**

Below: **Her Majesty The Queen visits the airport in the 1970s, with a familiar backdrop.**

Best of British

After World War Two, the then Labour Government announced plans to break up BOAC into three state-owned companies: BOAC, flying long haul routes including to North America; British South American Airways (BSAA), flying to South America and the Caribbean; and British European Airways (BEA), flying all domestic and all European routes.

BEA was founded on 1 January 1946 and operations commenced from Croydon and Northolt airports, with DH89A Dragon Rapides and Douglas DC-3s. It was tasked with making money from an untried network of air routes straggling across Europe. The links had to be scheduled services run regularly over unprofitable short distances, whatever the season. In those early days, all the airline had at its disposal was a handful of ex-RAF pilots, a collection of out-dated aircraft and very few maintenance and repair facilities. The post war depression squeezed the number of passengers to a minimum and BEA faced an uphill struggle to increase the market. The turning point came in 1950 when BEA made aviation history with the world's first turbine-powered commercial air service from London to Paris, using the UK Ministry of Supply-owned Vickers Viscount 630 prototype G-AHRF. By that time, BEA's main operating base at Northolt was the busiest airport in the UK, but the airline was still losing money. That changed with the appointment of Lord Douglas of Kirtleside as

chairman and Peter Masefield as managing director and the gradual shift of operations to the new international gateway of London (Heathrow) Airport.

Throughout the 1950s BEA expanded its European routes and introduced new aircraft, including the Airspeed Ambassador, which it called the Elizabethan and put it to work on its flagship 'Silver City' luxury service to Paris, complete with a level of passenger comfort that included caviar and cocktails! It boasted that its service was so smooth that no cocktails would be spilled!

BEA also ordered 20 Viscount 701s in August 1950 for delivery from 1953 and informed Vickers of its requirement for an aircraft with 10% lower costs per seat-mile than the 800 series Viscount. This provided the impetus for Vickers to begin developing the Vanguard high-capacity turboprop in 1953, which went on to provide valuable service with the airline.

During 1952, BEA carried its millionth passenger, and by the early 1960s it had become the western world's fifth-biggest passenger-carrying airline and the biggest outside the US. Some turnaround in fortunes. It's Heathrow base was now supported by massive engineering facilities that prepared it for its next step towards maintaining its dominance in the European skies, jet power. In 1960 BEA introduced its first jet aircraft, the short-haul Comet 4B and on 1 April 1964, it became the first to operate the DH121

*Above: **A new Elizabethan era was about to begin with the succession of Her Majesty the Queen, so BEA renamed its Airspeed Ambassador the 'Elizabethan'. Flying BEA's 'Silver Wing' service to Paris by Elizabethan became the most fashionable and elegant way of travelling. Each of the Elizabethans was named after a famous figure in the reign of Elizabeth 1, G-ALZS being 'William Shakespeare'.***

*Right: **BEA was still losing £1million a year, but the glamorous Elizabethan 'Silver Wing' service glossed over the fact. It was four miles a minute in a pressurised cabin and lunches of champagne, Scotch salmon and Cape pears in port. Breakfast in London and lunch in Paris cost £15.95 return, a princely sum in those days.***

Trident 1C, which a year later performed the world's first automatic landing during a scheduled commercial air service.

However, the good times were not to last. A government committee chaired by Sir Ronald Edwards published a report in 1969 called 'British Air Transport in the Seventies' arguing for the merger of BEA and BOAC. The findings were accepted by the then Conservative government and the British Airways Group was formed in September 1972 and the two airlines were officially merged on 1 April 1974. A BEA Trident operated the airline's final flight from Dublin to Heathrow on 31 March 1974. Following the late-night arrival at Heathrow at 23.30hrs of flight BE 943 (Bealine 943), BEA passed into history as the clock struck midnight.

PEAN AIRWAYS
G-ALZS
BEA
ROYAL MAIL

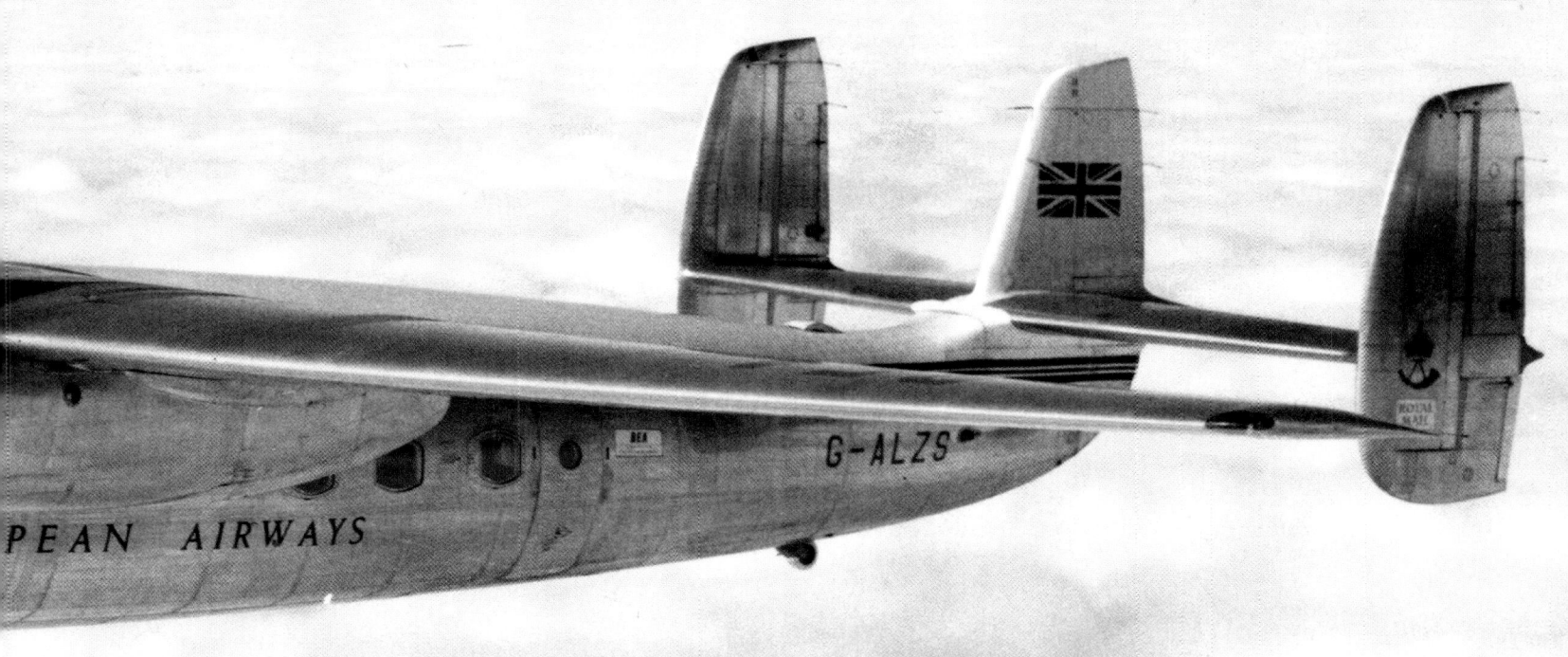

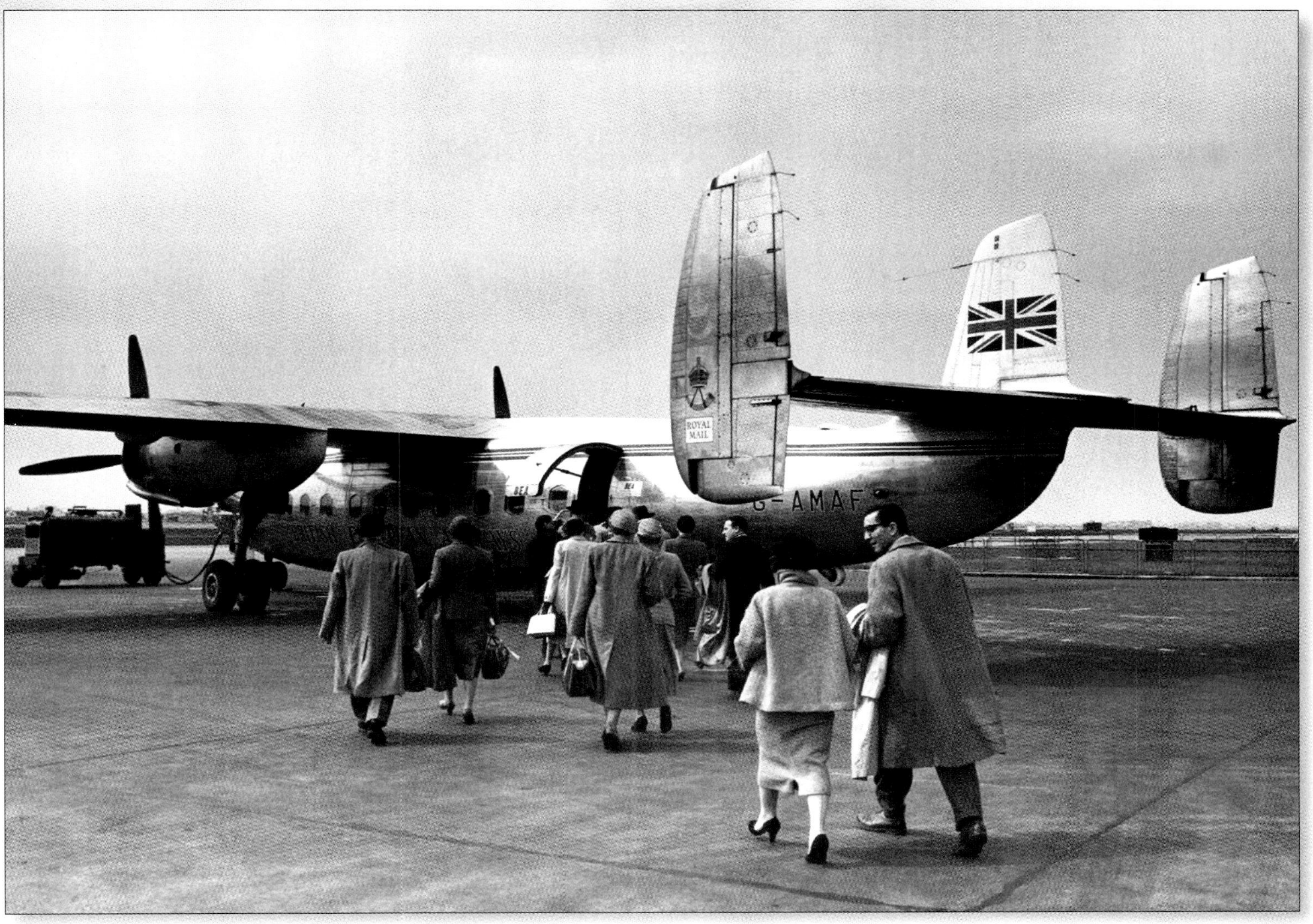
ROYAL MAIL
G-AMAF
BEA

This spread: The majestic Viscount was instrumental in the success of BEA, and vice versa. The prototype V700 (G-AMAV) made its first flight from Weybridge in BEA colours on 28 August. Regular passenger flights were launched by BEA in April 1953, the world's first scheduled turboprop airline service. BEA became a large user of the Viscount and by mid-1958 its fleet had carried over 2.75 million passengers over 200,000 flight hours. Following BEA's launch of the type, multiple independent charter operators such as British Eagle were quick to adopt the Viscount into their fleets.

BRITISH EUROPEAN AIRWAYS

G-AHRF

BEA

Right: Vanguard flying 1960's style was a very relaxed affair, though the boarding passengers at Heathrow Airport were sometimes exposed to the winter elements.

Below: BEA operated its first Vanguard schedule on 17 December 1960 from Heathrow to Paris. Following delivery of its full fleet of six V951 and 14 V953s by 30 March 1962, the type took over many of BEA's busier European and UK trunk routes. Initial seating was 18 first-class at the rear and 108 tourist, but this was changed to 139 all-tourist, in which configuration the Vanguard had very low operating costs per seat/mile. On flights up to 300 miles (480km), such as from London to Paris, Brussels and Amsterdam, the type could match the block times of the pure jets which were being introduced in the early 1960s. In the early 1970s most remaining BEA Vanguards were converted into freighters with a large forward cargo door, becoming the V953C Merchantman.

Left and below: **In March 1958 BEA entered the jet age when it ordered six short-haul versions of the Comet, the 4B variant, which featured a fuselage stretch of 38in and seating for 99 passengers. On 1 April 1960, BEA began commercial jet operations with its new Comet 4Bs. Soon it was flying jet operations from Heathrow to Athens, Istanbul, Moscow, Munich, Rome and Warsaw with an initial five-strong Comet fleet. By June, this fleet had grown to seven (out of an eventual 18) aircraft, enabling the launch of additional jet services to Copenhagen, Oslo, Stockholm, Düsseldorf, Malta, Zürich and Frankfurt.**

Bottom: **An aircraft synonymous with BEA is the Hawker Siddeley Trident. BEA's regular commercial Trident operations commenced on 1 April 1964, with its aircraft fitted in a 79-seat, two-class configuration, comprising 15 first class and 64 tourist class seats.**

*Top: **A BOAC Stratocruiser is dwarfed by the iconic hangar complex designed by Sir Owen Williams. The building remains in use today as a maintenance hangar with British Airways, though much of its exterior has been shrouded by extensions to accommodate later generations of airliners.***

*Above far left: **The vast expanse of newly-completed BEA Engineering base in 1954 that became home to the airline's fleet of Vikings, Viscounts and Elizabethans.***

*Above left: **Situated between the back-to-back BEA hangars, the maintenance section works on propellers for its fleet.***

*Left: **The cavernous interior of the BEA Engineering base swallowing up Viscounts a Viking and Elizabethans with ease.***

Maintaining the fleets

As the rapid postwar expansion of Heathrow gathered speed, so did the necessity to provide hangarage and engineering for the aircraft, particularly for those of the resident flagship carrier, BOAC.

From 1948 BOAC regarded the Stratocruiser as the best aircraft for its North Atlantic routes, but special new hangars would be needed to house the aircraft with their high tails and broad wingspan. The result was one of the most recognisable buildings at Heathrow, architect's Sir Owen Williams' iconic design that combined hangars with offices. The massive new Heathrow hangar block was completed in 1955 and in addition to its massive 188,000sq ft of hangarage, it also functioned as the corporation's HQ, housing some 4,000 staff. The imposing building was constructed of reinforced concrete throughout and was laid out with the hangars arranged in pairs back to back, with the main workshops between. The four hangar pens provided engineering space for the burgeoning fleet of Britannias, Comets, Stratocruisers and Constellations and were accessed by cavernous entrances, each 46ft high and 300ft wide. For many years, the building held the record for being the world's largest reinforced concrete structure.

With the transfer of BEA services from Northolt to Heathrow in the early-1950s, clearly the short-haul carrier needed its own engineering base to service its fleet of Vikings, Viscounts and Elizabethans. Work on the Heathrow site began in September 1950, and the first of the 10 hangar bays was opened in April 1952. The BEA engineering base comprised two large hangar buildings, each split into five bays, and each backed by a workshop building. Pre-stressed concrete was used extensively in the construction of both hangars and workshops, with the hangar roofs being of pressed aluminium sheeting. This vast complex was duly completed in 1954.

Meanwhile, the Wing Hangar at Heathrow was built for BOAC in 1954-56, opening in 1957. This was designed around the Bristol Britannia, the primary requirement being maintenance access to the wing, but modifications were soon made to accommodate the growing fleet of VC10s with its high T-tail arrangement.

In a testimony to the longevity of its design, the original Owen Williams hangar remains in use at Heathrow today, though with a number of extensions shrouding much of its identity.

Right: **A pair of BOAC Britannias being serviced in the Owen Williams-designed hangar that is still in use today.**

Below: **Boeing 707 undergoing engine test runs outside the main BOAC building at Heathrow. The first generation of turbojet aircraft made Heathrow a very noisy place indeed.**

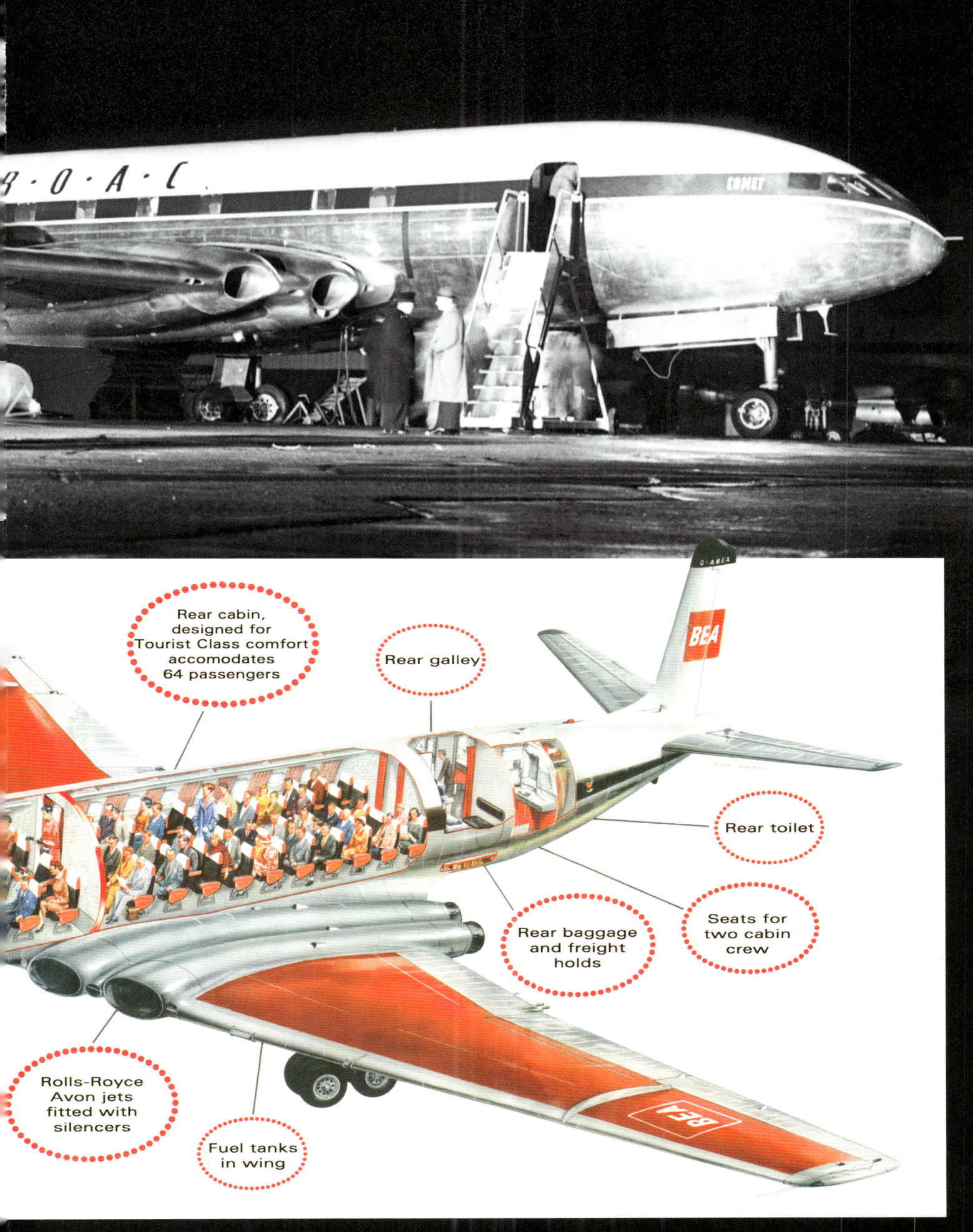

Rear cabin, designed for Tourist Class comfort accomodates 64 passengers

Rear galley

Rear toilet

Seats for two cabin crew

Rear baggage and freight holds

Rolls-Royce Avon jets fitted with silencers

Fuel tanks in wing

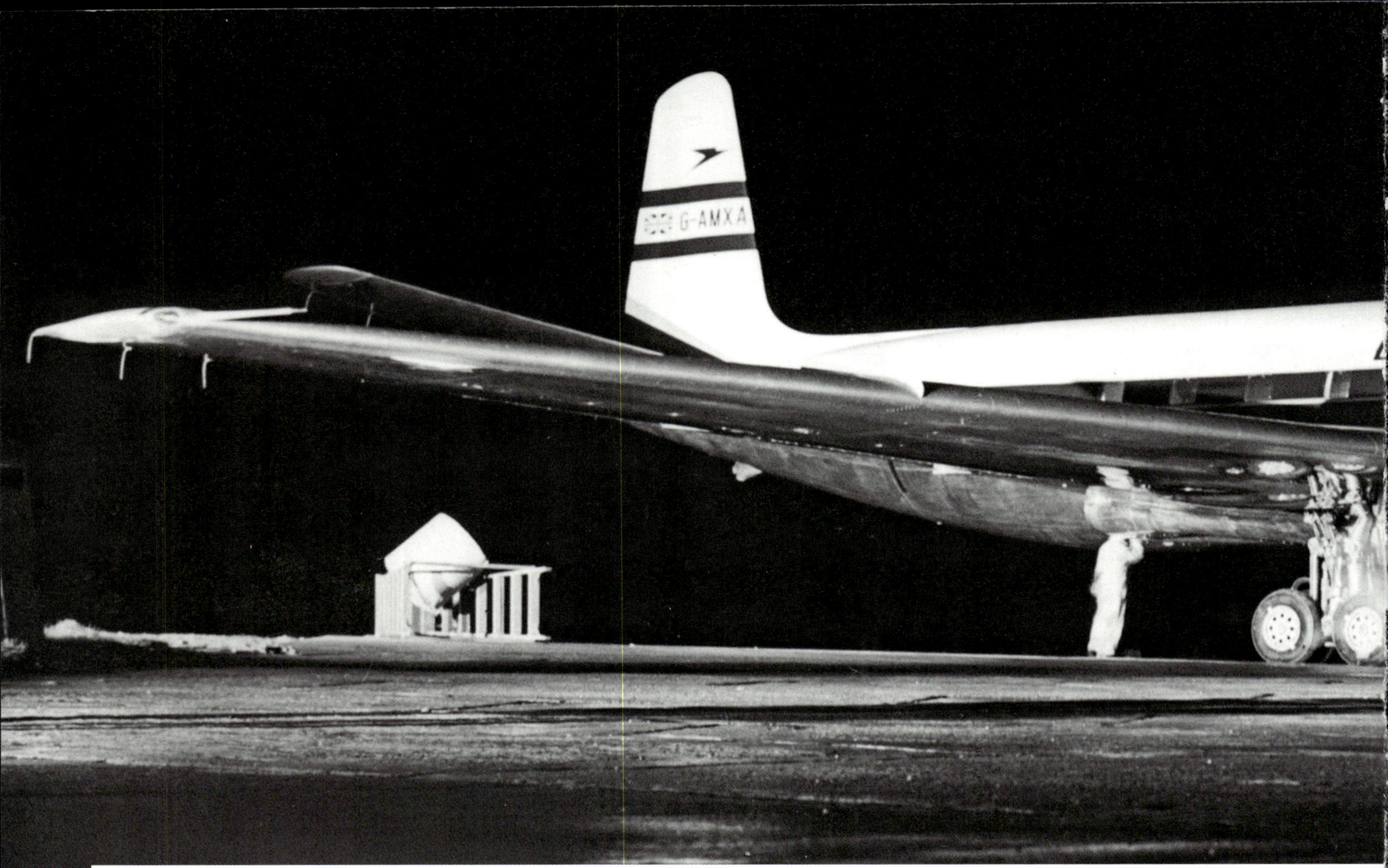
G-AMXA

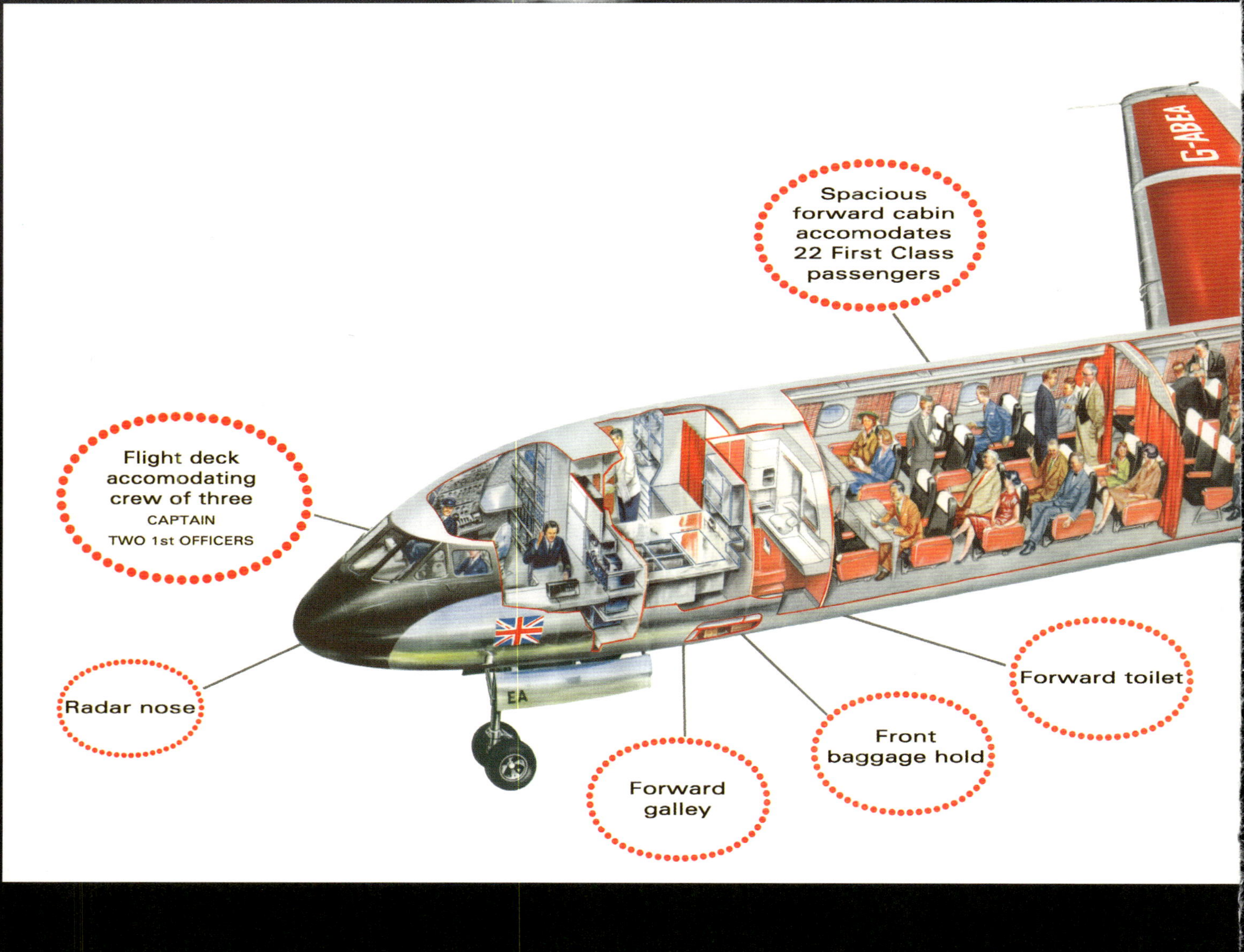
G-ABEA
Spacious forward cabin accomodates 22 First Class passengers
Flight deck accomodating crew of three
CAPTAIN
TWO 1st OFFICERS
Radar nose
Forward galley
Front baggage hold
Forward toilet

Blazing the trail

The tragic story of the Comet is well-known. As the world's first jet airliner to enter service on 2 May 1952, de Havilland and BOAC triumphantly changed the world of aviation overnight. But the glory was short-lived and the revolutionary jetliner was grounded after a series of unexplained tragic crashes. Metal fatigue was to blame and the aircraft returned stronger and better, but the lead had now been lost to the Americans and was never to be regained.

In an era of technological firsts, it was a matter of great national pride that Britain pioneered the way in jet airliner services. When the revolutionary de Havilland Comet first took to the air, its sleek clean lines pointed to an exciting future. Jets offered significant advantages over their propeller-driven counterparts, they were quicker, smoother, could fly higher and would revolutionise how passengers thought about air travel. Moreover,

Top left: A rare shot of Comet 2, G-AMXA, in BOAC livery, before the aircraft was transferred to the RAF for a military career. The Comet 2 never saw service with the airline as a result of the crashes, but paved the way for the updated and much revised Comet 4.

Left: A publicity leaflet released in 1960 showing the benefits of travel on a BEA Comet 4B.

Below: The sleek clean lines of one of BOAC's first Comet 1s, G-ALYX, look incongruous against the 'dated' setting of Heathrow's north side.

they had the potential to be more economical and earn the airlines more money. Thus it was with great fanfare that BOAC introduced its shiny new fleet of Comets onto its long-haul routes, with the promise of making the world a smaller place. Inevitably there were a few teething problems associated with the pioneering services, but Britain's lead in jet travel was assured. All this came to a tragic halt on the first anniversary of operations when G-ALYV was lost over India with all those on board. The accident enquiry found that structural failure had been sustained as a result of flying through a severe thunderstorm. Meanwhile the improved Comet 2 had flown and BOAC quickly placed an order for more. But disaster struck again on 10 January 1954 when Comet 1 G-ALYP broke up over the Mediterranean, again with the loss of all on board. Three months later G-ALYY also disappeared over the Mediterranean and this time the Comet fleet was grounded. As history recalls, the crashes were eventually traced to a fatigue failure of the pressure cabin, starting at a corner of one of the small windows. This led to a catastrophic break-up of the aircraft mid-air. As a result, the Comet was extensively redesigned with oval windows, structural reinforcement and other changes. Meanwhile, rival manufacturers had heeded the lessons learned from the Comet while developing their own aircraft.

Although sales never fully recovered, the improved Comet 2 and the prototype Comet 3

culminated in the redesigned Comet 4 series, which debuted in 1958. In those days, being the first airline to operate jet services between London and New York was a big deal and BOAC saw this as an opportunity to restore the Comet's reputation. In the pre-jet era passengers lumbered across the Atlantic at little more than 300mph. The elegant Lockheed Constellation could make 340mph at best, while the two-decked Stratocruiser cruised at 300mph. Jets promised speeds of 500mph-plus. Pan-American had been promising that it would be the first airline to mount 'pure' turbojet services across the Atlantic with its newly-delivered Boeing 707s, but Sir Gerard d'Erlanger, chairman of BOAC, had different ideas. On 3 October 1958, BOAC issued a sudden announcement that the New York Port Authority had given the British airline permission to begin jet operations. Thus, the next day two new Comet 4s inaugurated transatlantic services. One took off from London and refuelled at the Canadian staging post of Gander on Newfoundland before carrying on to New York. A second aircraft flew from New York's Idlewild Airport (later renamed John F. Kennedy International Airport) to London. The east-bound Comet, aided by strong tailwinds, did not require refuelling and made the journey in one hop.

BOAC would go on to dominate the London-New York route in the 1960s and early 1970s with Pan Am, but when it came to airliners the Americans were the long-term winners. The

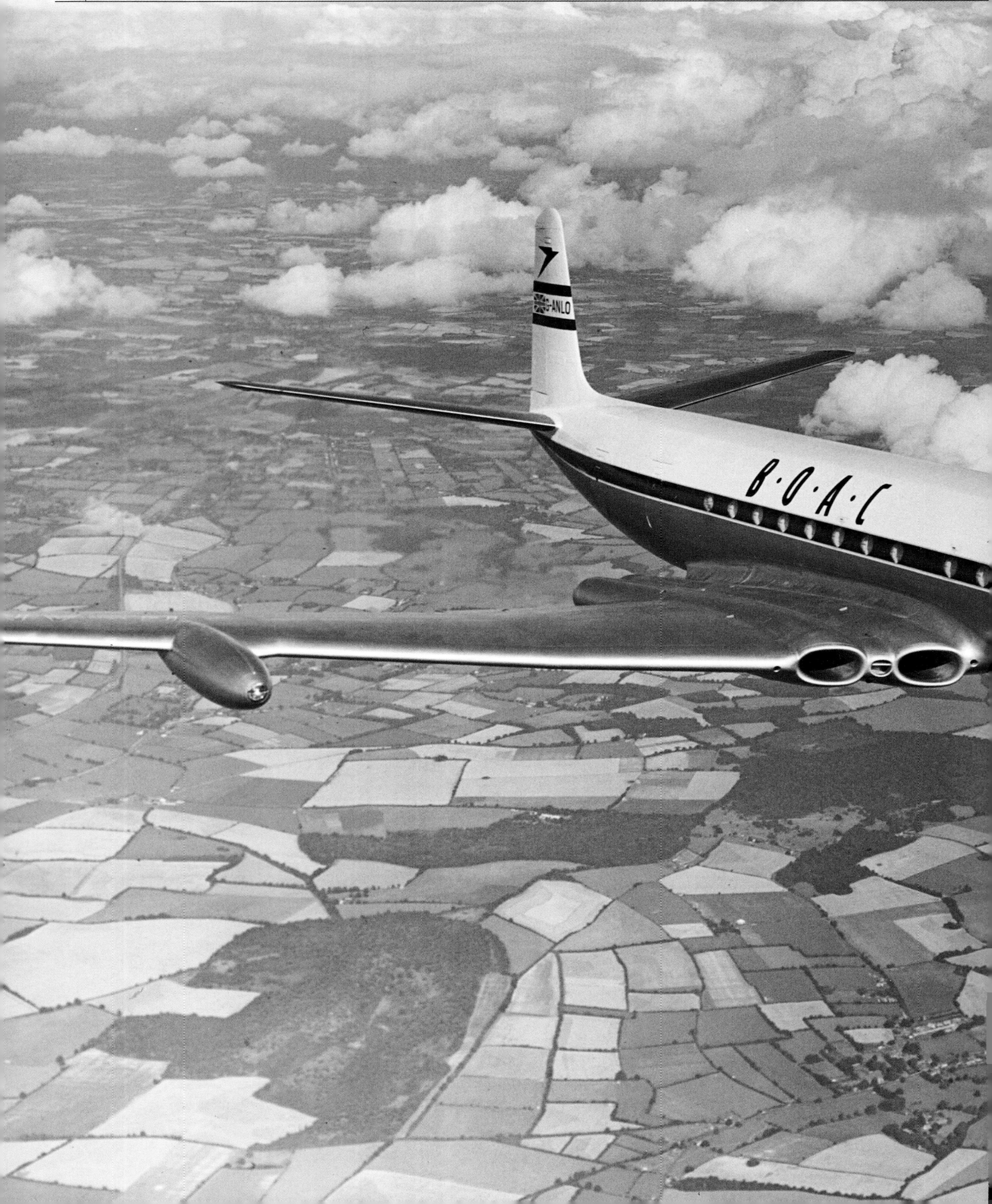
G-ANLO
B.O.A.C

Comet, with its limited passenger capacity, was no match for the larger, faster and more cost-effective Boeing 707 and its other US rival, the Douglas DC-8. After analysing route structures for the Comet, BOAC had reluctantly cast about for a successor and in 1956 entered into an agreement with Boeing to purchase the 707. In 1959 BOAC began shifting its Comets from transatlantic routes and released the Comet to associate companies, making the Comet 4's ascendancy as a premier airliner brief. Besides the 707 and DC-8, the introduction of the Vickers VC10 allowed competing aircraft to assume the high-speed, long-range passenger service role pioneered by the Comet. Within a few years the Comet was gone from BOAC service.

Meanwhile, on 7 November 1959, BEA took delivery of its first Comet 4Bs (G-APMB), nearly two months ahead of the contracted delivery on 1 January 1960. This was followed by the official handover ceremony of the airline's first jet airliner on 16 November. The 4B was designed specifically for BEA, to service its shorter range routes. It featured a slightly extended fuselage to seat up to 99 passengers and slightly shorter wings with no fuel tank pods. The only other airline to order the 4B was Olympic (for two), but in the event only 18 Comet 4Bs were built. This special short-haul version of the Comet was BEA's answer to the impending introduction of the Sud-Est Caravelle, Air France's new short-/medium-range jet, on the French flag carrier's European, North African and Middle Eastern network, including the prime Heathrow - Le Bourget route. BEA commenced jet operations from Heathrow to Athens, Istanbul, Moscow, Munich, Rome and Warsaw with an initial, five-strong Comet fleet.

BEA's Comet fleet gave good service throughout the 1960s, but the carrier had already turned its eyes to the next-generation of jet airliners. BEA flew its last scheduled Comet services in June 1969, the type thereafter being replaced by Tridents.

*Left: **Another Comet seen in BOAC livery that never made it to commercial service was the sole Comet 3, G-ANLO. It flew for the first time on 19 July 1954 and was a Comet 2 lengthened by 15ft 5in (4.70m) and powered by Avon M502s. The variant added wing pinion tanks, and offered greater capacity and range. The Comet 3 was destined to remain a development series since it did not incorporate the fuselage-strengthening modifications of the later series aircraft, and was not able to be fully pressurised. However, in BOAC colours, G-ANLO was flown by John Cunningham in a marathon round-the-world promotional tour in December 1955.***

Left: The compact cockpit interior of BOAC Comet 4, G-APDB.

Right: BEA's first Comet 4B G-APMB entered service in 1960. By June 1960 its fleet had grown to seven (out of an eventual 18) aircraft, enabling the launch of additional jet services to Copenhagen, Oslo, Stockholm, Düsseldorf, Malta, Zürich and Frankfurt.

Far right: A typical scene at Heathrow in the 1960s with three BEA Comet 4Bs parked on the apron, while a BEA Vanguard thunders overhead. Few would argue that the Comet was a fine looking airliner.

Below: Iconic Heathrow at its best with Speedbirds galore. BOAC Comet 4 G-APDM parked in front of the company hangars and offices. Delivered in April 1959, 'Delta Mike' served with the airline for nearly 10 years before it was leased to Malaysian airlines. Ultimately it was operated by Dan-Air.

Speedbird spirit

With its iconic 'Speedbird' logo and its central role in the glamorous 'jet age' of the 1950s and 1960s, BOAC has a romantic legacy. This true British institution dragged the nation out of the post war depression and flew the flag to the farthest-flung parts of the globe, acting as an unofficial ambassador for the country and its aircraft industry. Its brand spoke of unrivalled quality, but in reality the airline's dominating position had put a stranglehold on the industry.

The British Overseas Airways Corporation (BOAC for short) was created on 24 November 1939 from the merger of Imperial Airways and British Airways Ltd. As the British state airline, BOAC kept wartime Britain connected with its colonies and its allies, often operating under enemy fire. When peacetime returned, BOAC

was left with a fleet of outdated equipment, including lend-lease Douglas DC-3s, Liberators, converted Sunderlands, and the first Avro Lancastrians, Avro Yorks, and Handley Page Haltons. The Corporation's aircraft, bases and personnel were scattered worldwide, and it would take a decade to centralise its operations at Heathrow.

Back in 1943, the Brabazon Committee had laid down a set of civil aircraft transport types for the British aircraft industry to produce, but these were to be several years in coming,

Below: ***Immortalised in stone, Alcock and Brown look on enviously at their legacy, one of BOAC's fleet of Boeing 707s that brought mass travel to long-haul routes. G-APFC was one of the first received by the airline when it was handed over in 1960. Following a long career it was transferred to British Airways.***

and often not what BOAC wanted or needed. Reluctantly, to remain competitive with American carriers plying the lucrative Atlantic routes, BOAC was given permission to purchase Constellations and then Stratocruisers, the latter offering a double-deck non-stop eastbound service from New York City to London from October 1949.

As the national airline BOAC was also expected to be the launch customer for new British airliners, including the Avro Tudor, Handley Page Hermes, Bristol Britannia and, much later, the Vickers VC10. Unfortunately these designs ended up being so closely tailored to BOAC's specifications, that they achieved very few export sales, leaving the market clear for US domination.

Meanwhile, the Hermes and Canadair DC-4M Argonaut joined the BOAC fleet between

1949 and 1950, replacing the last of the non-pressurised types on passenger services. When service entry of the Bristol Britannia was delayed in late 1956, BOAC was permitted to purchase 10 new Douglas DC-7Cs. These long range aircraft enabled BOAC to operate non-stop westbound flights from London and Manchester to New York and other US East Coast destinations.

The 1950's were a 'golden age' for BOAC, the highlight being in May 1952 when it was the first airline to introduce jet airliner services with its de Havilland Comet. The revolutionary new design slashed flying times around the globe but, as related elsewhere, the euphoria was to be short-lived.

This was also the age of the turboprop and BOAC had placed much faith in the Bristol Britannia to maintain its commercial success across the Atlantic. However, serious delays in its development rendered it obsolete even before it entered service.

BOAC had never lost faith in the de Havilland Comet and reintroduced the much-modified

Comet 4 in October 1958, becoming the first airline to operate jet services on the prestigious London-New York route. But by then the airliner industry had moved on and Boeing was in the ascendancy with its long-range large capacity Boeing 707.

In order to keep pace with its rival airlines, in October 1956 BOAC ordered 15 Boeing 707s with Rolls-Royce Conway engines, for entry into service in 1960. Sir Giles Guthrie, who took charge of BOAC in 1964, preferred the Boeing aircraft for economic reasons. However, after a row in Parliament the government instructed BOAC to purchase 17 Vickers VC10 aircraft from a 30-aircraft order which Guthrie had cancelled. The Standard VC10 had higher operating costs than the 707, largely due to BOAC's requirement at the design stage for the aircraft to have excellent hot and high performance for Commonwealth (African/Asian) routes, but the larger Super VC10 was a success with passengers on the North Atlantic and maintained BOAC's market position on the North Atlantic until the introduction of the

game-changing wide-bodied Boeing 747 at the beginning of the 1970s. The carrier went on to become the biggest operator of the 'jumbo' outside of the US.

In just 25 short years, aviation travel had gone from being the domain of the elite, to travel for the masses. The world had been revolutionised and BOAC was at the forefront of it all. But pressure to introduce economies and improve efficiency in Britain's two state-owned airlines lead to the establishment of a unified British Airways. By 1 April 1974 the amalgamation with BEA was finally complete and BOAC had flown into history.

Thus, BOAC ceased to exist on the eve of supersonic travel, but in a last act of defiance the first Concorde delivered to British Airways carried the registration G-BOAC. The Speedbird legacy had lived on after all.

Far left: Avro Yorks, such as G-AGSP, played an important role in the immediate postwar services of BOAC. This aircraft was delivered in May 1946 and served with the airline for nearly 10 years before it was broken up in 1955.

Left: The elegant Lockheed L-049 Constellation brought undisputed glamour to BOAC's long-haul services. This aircraft is G-AKCE which was delivered in 1947 and is seen at Heathrow in 1954, shortly before it was sold to Capital Airlines as N2741A.

Below left: Framed by the tail of a KLM Constellation, Stratocruiser G-AKGH 'Caledonia' was the first to be delivered to BOAC when it was handed over in November 1949. The airline was to eventually operate 17 of the type in the 1950s, and advertised their services with suitable advertising posters from the era. At the time the BOAC London-New York return fare was $630, unaffordable for most.

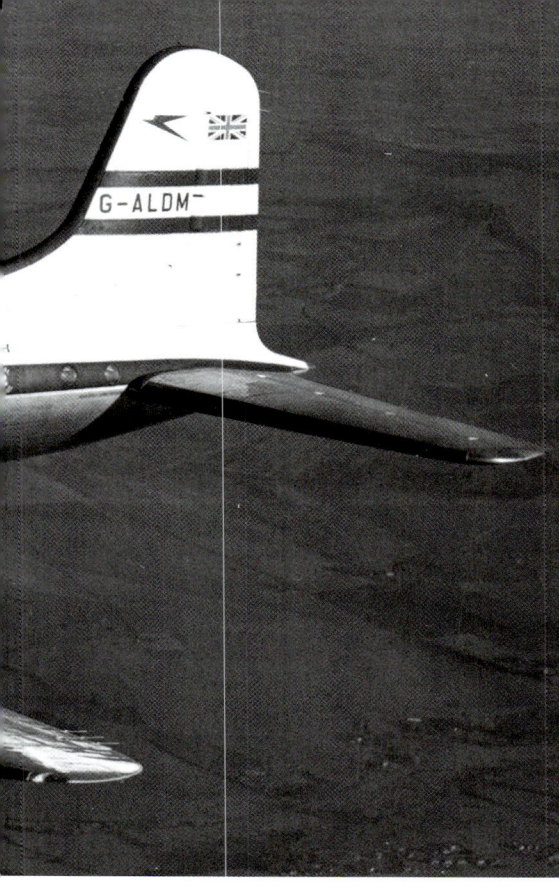

Left: **The entry of the Handley Page Hermes into BOAC service was so delayed that by the time deliveries commenced its planned replacement, the Canadair Argonaut, was already in operation. Nevertheless the Hermes fleet was based at London and initially replaced the Solent flying-boats on the four-times weekly London-Rome-Cairo-Khartoum-Nairobi route. It continued to fly on BOAC's African routes, but the type was withdrawn from service after the airline started to receive the more economical Comet 1s. The type had a brief reprieve on East African routes following the grounding of the Comet, but the Hermes was finally withdrawn from BOAC on 4 December 1954 and its fleet sold off at a capital loss of £3 million.**

Bottom left: **The Britannia, or 'Whispering Giant' as it was often called, was popular with its passengers, but sadly the age of the jet airliner was already nigh by the time it entered service and it was soon viewed as outdated. The main long-range versions were the srs 310s, of which BOAC took 18 and put them into service between London and New York from September 1957. By March 1964 BOAC owned 50 of the type, 10 being Britannia 312s. BOAC's last scheduled Britannia flight was April 1965.**

Inset left: **The first Bristol Britannia srs102 for BOAC, G-ANBA, was finally delivered on 22 August 1957.** *Andy Hay/Flyingart*

Bottom right: **After the much-publicised grounding of the Comet 1, BOAC kept faith with de Havilland and ordered a fleet of much-improved and developed Comet 4s, including G-APDR pictured here. By doing so they were able to inaugurate the world's first transatlantic scheduled jet services in 1958, much to the chagrin of Pan-American. However, in reality the larger Boeing 707 was a much better fit for the route and it was not long before the Comet was 'relegated' to a less prestigious role.**

Inset right: **Trail blazers. The de Havilland Comet and BOAC will forever be remembered for pioneering jet airliner operations.** *Andy Hay/Flyingart*

Far left: **Heathrow in the swinging sixties with Boeing 707s dominating the scene in front of the carrier's HQ building. One can only imagine the decibel levels that echoed around Heathrow at this time.**

Inset left: **The timeless blue and gold livery of BOAC was integral in projecting a message of class and quality to the world. G-APFD was the first Boeing 707 received by the airline in April 1960 and was eventually sold to BEA Airtours in February 1973.** Andy Hay/Flyingart

Left: **The sweeping beauty of the Vickers VC10. A total of 12 standard VC10s was purchased in 1964–65, followed by 17 stretched Super VC10s in 1965–69. The VC10 became an immensely popular aircraft in the BOAC fleet, both with passengers and crew, being particularly praised for its comfort and low cabin noise level. To this day, the VC10 holds the record of being the fastest sub-sonic airliner ever built.**

Below: **When the giant wide-body Boeing 747 entered BOAC service in 1970, airliner travel was totally redefined. Affordable air travel was now available for all and the world became a smaller place overnight.**

Trident misfit

The Hawker Siddeley Trident holds a pioneering place in aviation history on a number of counts. It was the first T-tail rear-engined three-engined jet airliner to be designed. It performed the world's first automatic touchdown on a commercial flight with fare-paying passengers and performed the world's first fully automatic landing in fog by a civil aircraft in zero visibility. Sadly the rest of its career was not such a qualified success…

The story of the Hawker Siddeley Trident began in 1956 when de Havilland designed the DH121 in response to a call by the state-owned British European Airways Corporation (BEA) for a jet airliner for its premier West European routes. The airline's requirements fluctuated greatly in the 1950s and a decade later evolved radically away from the original Trident concept. Adherence to BEA's changing specification was widely seen as limiting the Trident's appeal to other airlines and delaying its service entry.

The first Trident 1C entered service with BEA in 1964, having first flown in 1962. The Trident performed well and was reliable, but BEA soon realised that it required a larger aircraft. Hawker Siddeley responded first with the 1E variant, primarily for the export market, and the 2E for BEA, featuring uprated engines, larger wing span, improved high lift devices (slats) and greater capacity and range.

One of the key features of the Trident was its ability to operate in virtually all weather conditions thanks to its Auto-land/blind landing system and it pioneered the operational introduction of the technology.

Meanwhile, BEA was still insistent that it needed a bigger medium-range airliner, but the government was equally insistent that it should 'buy British'. The result was the introduction of the Trident 3B. A fuselage stretch of 5m (16ft 5in) made room for up to 180 passengers, raised the gross weight to 143,000lb (65,000kg), and modifications were made to the wing to increase its chord. However, BEA was concerned that the aircraft would not be able to perform adequately in 'hot and high' conditions, in light of such issues experienced on the Trident 2E. Since its Rolls-Royce Spey 512s were the last of the Spey line, extra power would be difficult to add. Instead of attempting to replace the three engines, Hawker Siddeley decided to add a fourth engine in the tail, the tiny RB162 turbojet, fed from its own intake behind a pair of movable doors. The engine added 15% more thrust for take-off, while adding only 5% more weight, and would only be used when needed. BEA accepted this as the Trident 3B, and ordered 26.

Popular with its passengers, Tridents continued to serve with BEA until its successor, British Airways, began retiring the oldest aircraft in 1976 with the final 3Bs retiring in 1985.

Right: **Tailor-made for short-medium haul services on BEA's extensive European network, by the time the Trident had entered service with the airline in 1964, the airline wanted an aircraft with larger capacity to compete with its rivals. This Trident 1, G-ARPC, was one of the early deliveries, but was damaged beyond repair at Heathrow when a cabin fire broke out while it was on stand in late December 1975. Thankfully there were no casualties**

Below: **Hands free, 1960's style. A Trident crew show complete faith in the aircraft's automatic landing system.**

*Left: **Heyday of the BEA Trident, with nine of the type lined up at a busy Heathrow in the early 1970s. The Trident Threes can be identified on the line by their larger auxiliary engines mounted at the rear base of the tailfin.***

*Below left: **Trident Two G-AVFC, undergoing servicing in the pristine BEA maintenance facilities at Heathrow.***

*Above: **Tragedy struck the BEA fleet on 18 June 1972 when Flight 548, Trident 1 G-ARPI, stalled due to pilot error and crashed at Staines shortly after take-off from Heathrow Airport. All 118 on board were killed. As of 2016, it is still the worst aviation accident to have occurred on British soil. While technically advanced, the Trident (and other aircraft with a T-tail arrangement) had potentially dangerous stalling characteristics. If its airspeed was insufficient, and particularly if its high-lift devices were not extended at the low speeds typical of climbing away after take-off or of approaching to land, it could enter a deep stall from which recovery was practically impossible. The incident resulted in the Trident being fitted with an automatic stall warning system known as a 'stick shaker', and a stall recovery system known as a 'stick pusher' which automatically pitched the aircraft down to build up speed if the crew failed to respond to the warning.***

*Below: **These were the type of conditions that the Trident excelled in.. and often encountered at Heathrow, an airport notorious for fog.***

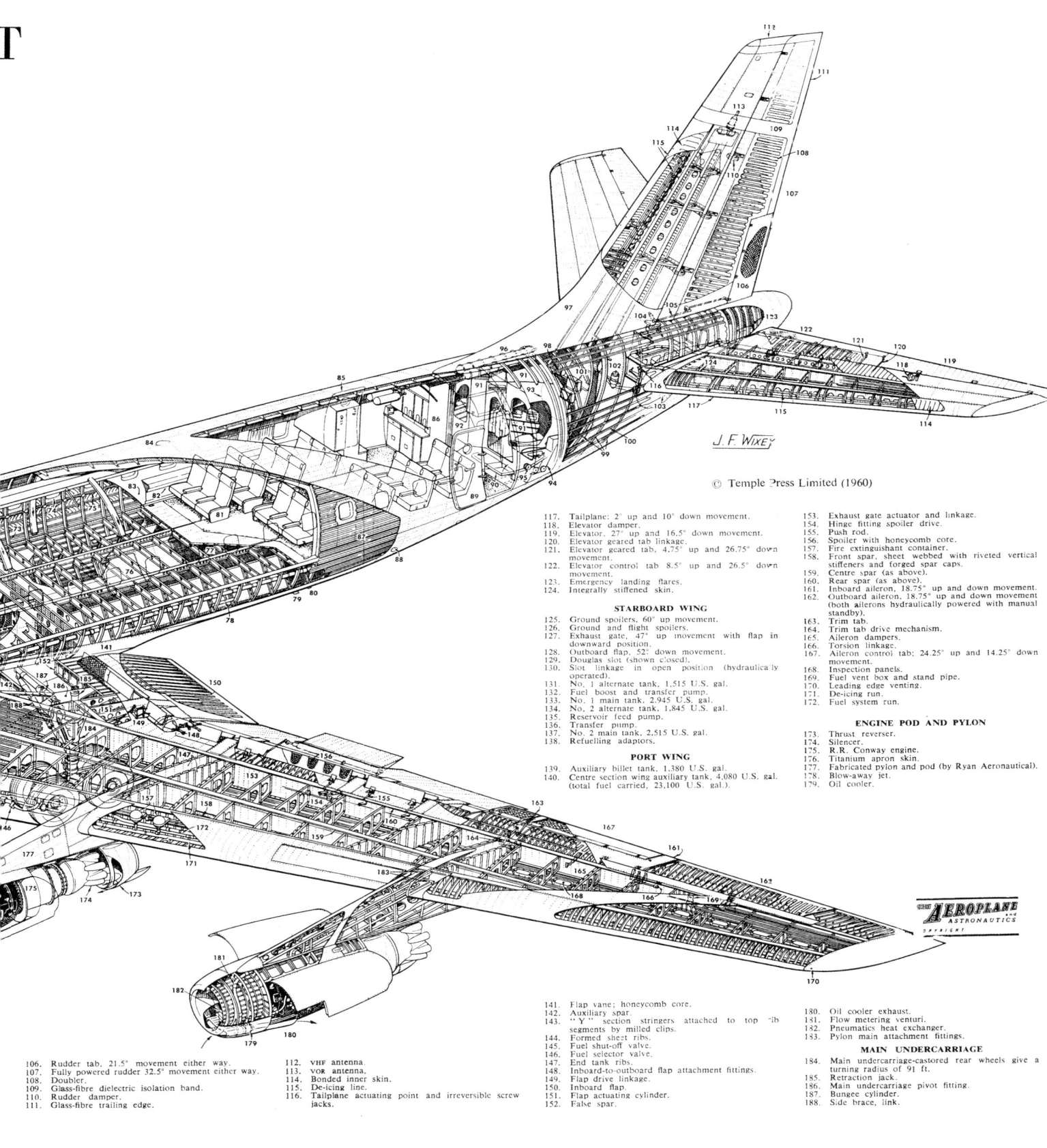

T

J. F. WIXEY

© Temple Press Limited (1960)

THE AEROPLANE
AND ASTRONAUTICS
COPYRIGHT

117. Tailplane: 2° up and 10° down movement.
118. Elevator damper.
119. Elevator, 27° up and 16.5° down movement.
120. Elevator geared tab linkage.
121. Elevator geared tab, 4.75° up and 26.75° down movement.
122. Elevator control tab 8.5° up and 26.5° down movement.
123. Emergency landing flares.
124. Integrally stiffened skin.

STARBOARD WING

125. Ground spoilers, 60° up movement.
126. Ground and flight spoilers.
127. Exhaust gate, 47° up movement with flap in downward position.
128. Outboard flap, 52° down movement.
129. Douglas slot (shown closed).
130. Slot linkage in open position (hydraulically operated).
131. No. 1 alternate tank, 1,515 U.S. gal.
132. Fuel boost and transfer pump.
133. No. 1 main tank, 2,945 U.S. gal.
134. No. 2 alternate tank, 1,845 U.S. gal.
135. Reservoir feed pump.
136. Transfer pump.
137. No. 2 main tank, 2,515 U.S. gal.
138. Refuelling adaptors.

PORT WING

139. Auxiliary billet tank, 1,380 U.S. gal.
140. Centre section wing auxiliary tank, 4,080 U.S. gal. (total fuel carried, 23,100 U.S. gal.).

153. Exhaust gate actuator and linkage.
154. Hinge fitting spoiler drive.
155. Push rod.
156. Spoiler with honeycomb core.
157. Fire extinguishant container.
158. Front spar, sheet webbed with riveted vertical stiffeners and forged spar caps.
159. Centre spar (as above).
160. Rear spar (as above).
161. Inboard aileron, 18.75° up and down movement.
162. Outboard aileron, 18.75° up and down movement (both ailerons hydraulically powered with manual standby).
163. Trim tab.
164. Trim tab drive mechanism.
165. Aileron dampers.
166. Torsion linkage.
167. Aileron control tab: 24.25° up and 14.25° down movement.
168. Inspection panels.
169. Fuel vent box and stand pipe.
170. Leading edge venting.
171. De-icing run.
172. Fuel system run.

ENGINE POD AND PYLON

173. Thrust reverser.
174. Silencer.
175. R.R. Conway engine.
176. Titanium apron skin.
177. Fabricated pylon and pod (by Ryan Aeronautical).
178. Blow-away jet.
179. Oil cooler.

141. Flap vane; honeycomb core.
142. Auxiliary spar.
143. "Y" section stringers attached to top rib segments by milled clips.
144. Formed sheet ribs.
145. Fuel shut-off valve.
146. Fuel selector valve.
147. End tank ribs.
148. Inboard-to-outboard flap attachment fittings.
149. Flap drive linkage.
150. Inboard flap.
151. Flap actuating cylinder.
152. False spar.

180. Oil cooler exhaust.
181. Flow metering venturi.
182. Pneumatics heat exchanger.
183. Pylon main attachment fittings.

MAIN UNDERCARRIAGE

184. Main undercarriage-castored rear wheels give a turning radius of 91 ft.
185. Retraction jack.
186. Main undercarriage pivot fitting.
187. Bungee cylinder.
188. Side brace, link.

106. Rudder tab, 21.5° movement either way.
107. Fully powered rudder 32.5° movement either way.
108. Doubler.
109. Glass-fibre dielectric isolation band.
110. Rudder damper.
111. Glass-fibre trailing edge.

112. VHF antenna.
113. VOR antenna.
114. Bonded inner skin.
115. De-icing line.
116. Tailplane actuating point and irreversible screw jacks.

HAWKER SIDDELEY TRIDENT 1E

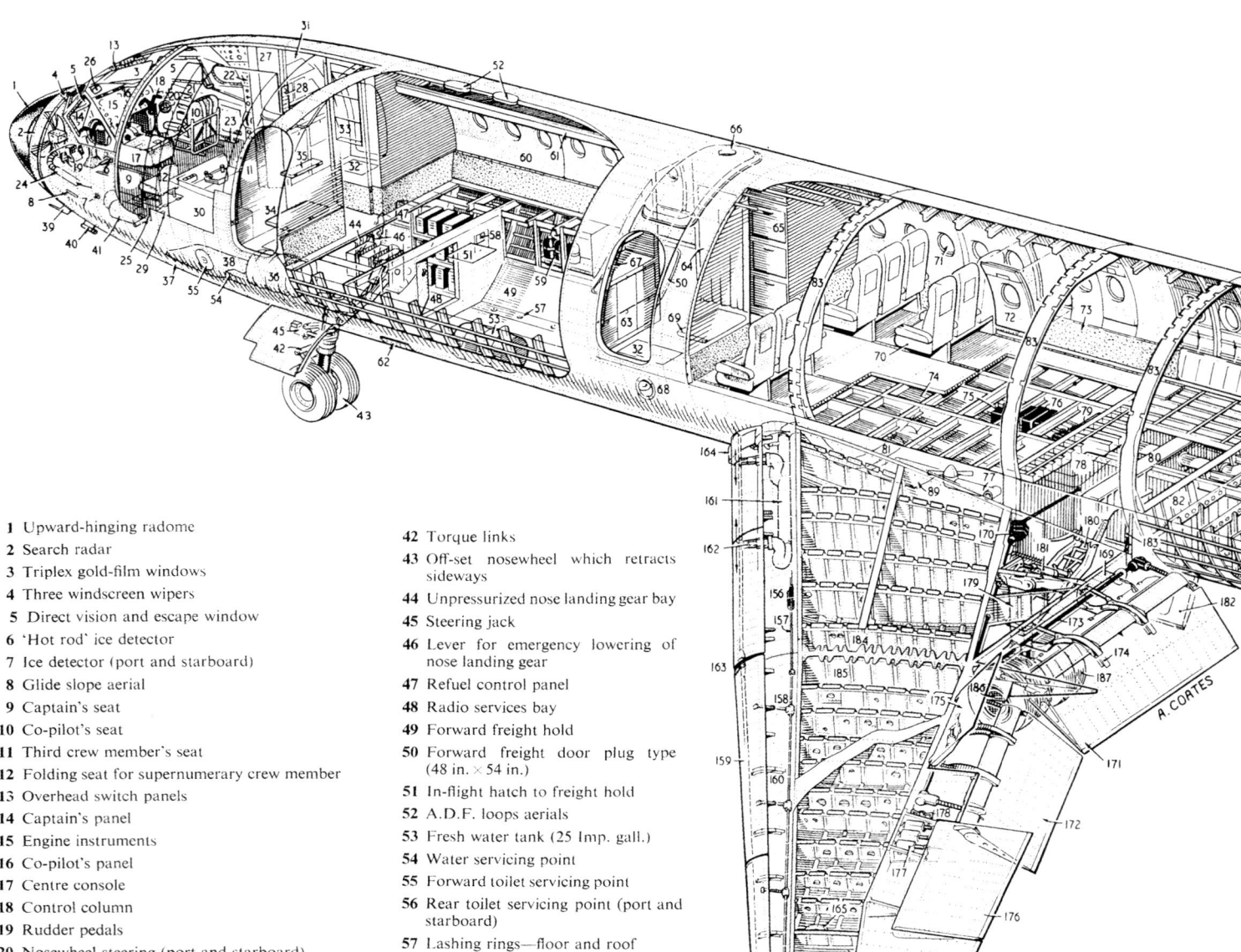

1 Upward-hinging radome
2 Search radar
3 Triplex gold-film windows
4 Three windscreen wipers
5 Direct vision and escape window
6 'Hot rod' ice detector
7 Ice detector (port and starboard)
8 Glide slope aerial
9 Captain's seat
10 Co-pilot's seat
11 Third crew member's seat
12 Folding seat for supernumerary crew member
13 Overhead switch panels
14 Captain's panel
15 Engine instruments
16 Co-pilot's panel
17 Centre console
18 Control column
19 Rudder pedals
20 Nosewheel steering (port and starboard)
21 Miscellaneous stowages
22 Aircraft services station
23 Nose and main landing gear emergency controls
24 Foot warmer
25 Radio rack
26 Eyebrow windows
27 Main distribution panel
28 Main relay and steward's control panel
29 Crew wardrobe
30 Forward toilet
31 Forward galley
32 Emergency escape chutes
33 Book rack
34 Two folding seats for stewards
35 Folding shelf for stewards
36 Forward water tank
37 Control and electrical equipment bay
38 Access door to equipment bay
39 Pitot heads (2 off for A.D.C., 1 off for standby A.S.I.)
40 'Q' feel pitot-static head
41 'Q' feel unit

42 Torque links
43 Off-set nosewheel which retracts sideways
44 Unpressurized nose landing gear bay
45 Steering jack
46 Lever for emergency lowering of nose landing gear
47 Refuel control panel
48 Radio services bay
49 Forward freight hold
50 Forward freight door plug type (48 in. × 54 in.)
51 In-flight hatch to freight hold
52 A.D.F. loops aerials
53 Fresh water tank (25 Imp. gall.)
54 Water servicing point
55 Forward toilet servicing point
56 Rear toilet servicing point (port and starboard)
57 Lashing rings—floor and roof
58 Livestock compartment specially ventilated section when required
59 Three 2,100 litre portable gaseous oxygen sets
60 1st class compartment—4 seats abreast
61 Luggage racks housing passenger service panels
62 Static heads (port and starboard)
63 Mid-ships galley
64 Wardrobe
65 Food stowage
66 Centre passenger door (pull-in, up and over plug type)
67 Door support and slide rail
68 Wing icing inspection lamp
69 Two folding seats for stewards
70 Tourist compartment—6 seats abreast
71 Passenger windows (10 in. × 13.5 in.)
72 Escape hatches, 2 per side (Type III inward pull-in) (20 in. × 36 in.)
73 Air conditioning duct
74 Centre torsion box (fuel tank)
75 Fatigue meters

76 Yaw rate gyro
77 Emergency ram-air turbine
78 Main landing gear bays
79 Aileron non-linear gearing unit and autopilot
80 Main floor support beam
81 Wing anti-icing duct
82 Rear sloping landing gear bay pressure bulkhead
83 Machined wing fuselage frames
84 Rear freight hold
85 Rear freight door plug type (50 in. × 35 in.)
86 Compressed air for emergency operation of main landing gear
87 Rear toilet (port and starboard)

SHORT/MEDIUM-RANGE AIRLINER

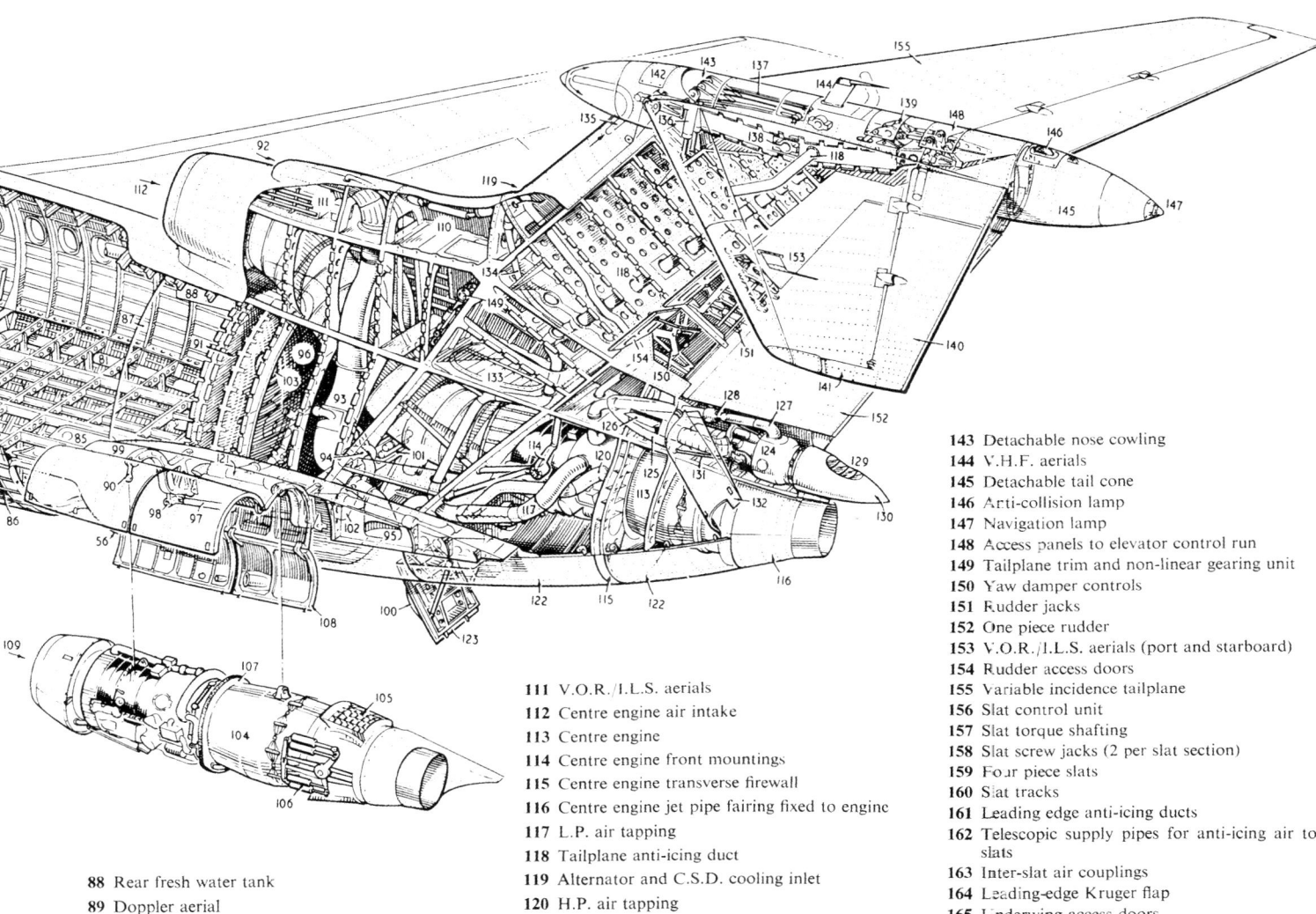

88 Rear fresh water tank
89 Doppler aerial
90 Pod engine mounting beams and frames
91 Air conditioning bay
92 Heat exchanger air inlet
93 Cabin air and heat exchanger
94 Cold air unit
95 Heat exchanger exhaust duct
96 Pressure dome
97 Thrust strut
98 Thrust trunnion
99 Fixed pod cowling
100 Bumper
101 Hydraulic bay
102 Hydraulic reservoirs (port and starboard)
103 Cabin pressure and safety valve outlet
104 Three Rolls-Royce Spey engines
105 Thrust reverser cascade (outers only)
106 Thrust reverser jacks
107 Firewalls
108 Engine access door
109 Anti-iced air intake
110 H.F. aerial

111 V.O.R./I.L.S. aerials
112 Centre engine air intake
113 Centre engine
114 Centre engine front mountings
115 Centre engine transverse firewall
116 Centre engine jet pipe fairing fixed to engine
117 L.P. air tapping
118 Tailplane anti-icing duct
119 Alternator and C.S.D. cooling inlet
120 H.P. air tapping
121 Main H.P. air supply duct
122 Centre engine access doors
123 Equipment bay access door with integral stairs and bumper
124 Auxiliary power unit
125 A.P.U. intake silencer and plenum chamber
126 A.P.U. intake doors
127 A.P.U. compressor feed to aircraft air system
128 Bleed dump valve
129 A.P.U. exhaust
130 Jet pipe fairing
131 A.P.U. mounting
132 A.P.U. access doors
133 Space for water injection tank
134 Anti-icing for leading edge of fin
135 Anti-icing for bullet nose
136 Tailplane jacks
137 Hydraulic pipes
138 Tailplane hinge bearings
139 Elevator linkage
140 Elevator
141 Mass balance
142 Access to tailplane jacks

143 Detachable nose cowling
144 V.H.F. aerials
145 Detachable tail cone
146 Anti-collision lamp
147 Navigation lamp
148 Access panels to elevator control run
149 Tailplane trim and non-linear gearing unit
150 Yaw damper controls
151 Rudder jacks
152 One piece rudder
153 V.O.R./I.L.S. aerials (port and starboard)
154 Rudder access doors
155 Variable incidence tailplane
156 Slat control unit
157 Slat torque shafting
158 Slat screw jacks (2 per slat section)
159 Four piece slats
160 Slat tracks
161 Leading edge anti-icing ducts
162 Telescopic supply pipes for anti-icing air to slats
163 Inter-slat air couplings
164 Leading-edge Kruger flap
165 Underwing access doors
166 Vent surge tank
167 Retractable landing lamp
168 Navigation lamp
169 Lift dumper
170 Hydraulic motor for flap operation
171 Inner double-slotted flaps
172 Outer double-slotted flaps
173 Flap torque shafting
174 Flap tracks (2 per flap)
175 Air brake/spoiler
176 Aileron
177 Aileron jacks
178 Roll damper
179 Main landing gear leg
180 Side-stay assembly
181 Retraction jack
182 Main landing gear doors
183 Door jack
184 No. 1 fuel tank (port and starboard)
185 No. 2 fuel tank (port and starboard)
186 Brake cooling fan
187 Main gear wheels incorporating anti-skid disk brakes

THE DOUGLAS DC-8 TURBOJET TRANSPORT

Four Rolls-Royce Conway Turbojets

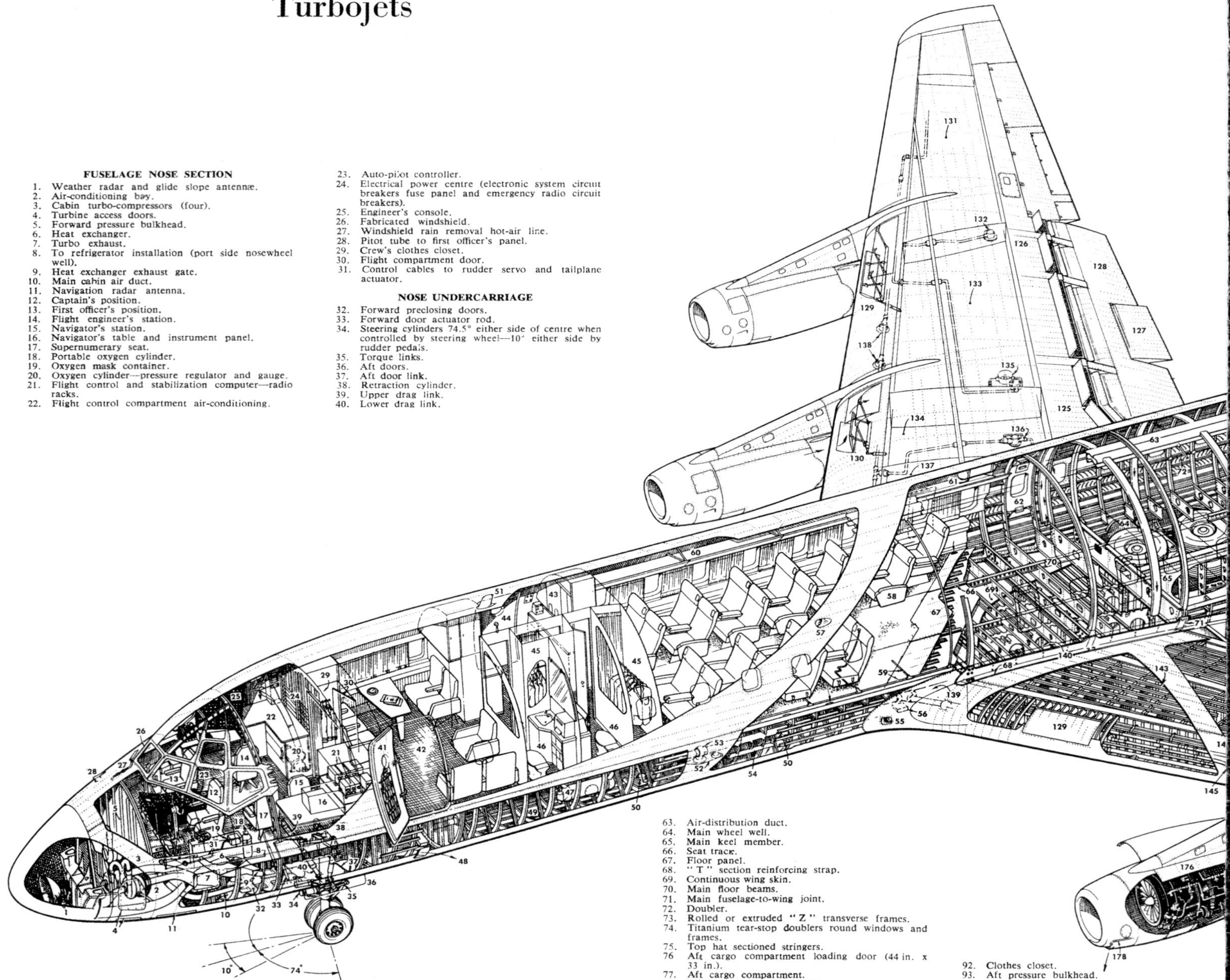

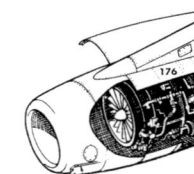

FUSELAGE NOSE SECTION

1. Weather radar and glide slope antennæ.
2. Air-conditioning bay.
3. Cabin turbo-compressors (four).
4. Turbine access doors.
5. Forward pressure bulkhead.
6. Heat exchanger.
7. Turbo exhaust.
8. To refrigerator installation (port side nosewheel well).
9. Heat exchanger exhaust gate.
10. Main cabin air duct.
11. Navigation radar antenna.
12. Captain's position.
13. First officer's position.
14. Flight engineer's station.
15. Navigator's station.
16. Navigator's table and instrument panel.
17. Supernumerary seat.
18. Portable oxygen cylinder.
19. Oxygen mask container.
20. Oxygen cylinder—pressure regulator and gauge.
21. Flight control and stabilization computer—radio racks.
22. Flight control compartment air-conditioning.
23. Auto-pilot controller.
24. Electrical power centre (electronic system circuit breakers fuse panel and emergency radio circuit breakers).
25. Engineer's console.
26. Fabricated windshield.
27. Windshield rain removal hot-air line.
28. Pitot tube to first officer's panel.
29. Crew's clothes closet.
30. Flight compartment door.
31. Control cables to rudder servo and tailplane actuator.

NOSE UNDERCARRIAGE

32. Forward preclosing doors.
33. Forward door actuator rod.
34. Steering cylinders 74.5° either side of centre when controlled by steering wheel—10° either side by rudder pedals.
35. Torque links.
36. Aft doors.
37. Aft door link.
38. Retraction cylinder.
39. Upper drag link.
40. Lower drag link.

LOUNGE AND FIRST-CLASS AREA

41. Forward plug-type entry door (72 in. x 34 in.).
42. Eight-seat lounge.
43. Forward galley.
44. Starboard forward galley service door (64 in. x 37 in.).
45. Clothes closet.
46. Toilet.
47. Toilet waste tank.
48. Refrigeration exhaust.
49. Forward cargo compartment.
50. "L" band antennæ.
51. VHF blade antenna.
52. ADF loop antenna.
53. Aft cabin blower.
54. Diffuser.
55. Landing light.
56. Marker beacon antenna.
57. Wing light.
58. Four-abreast de-luxe seating (22-in. aisle—40 seats).
59. Oxygen run.
60. Light luggage rack.
61. Emergency oxygen cylinder—pressure regulator and gauge.
62. Emergency exit doors 38 in. x 20 in. (two either side).

63. Air-distribution duct.
64. Main wheel well.
65. Main keel member.
66. Seat track.
67. Floor panel.
68. "T" section reinforcing strap.
69. Continuous wing skin.
70. Main floor beams.
71. Main fuselage-to-wing joint.
72. Doubler.
73. Rolled or extruded "Z" transverse frames.
74. Titanium tear-stop doublers round windows and frames.
75. Top hat sectioned stringers.
76. Aft cargo compartment loading door (44 in. x 33 in.).
77. Aft cargo compartment.
78. Diffuser under-floor airflow.
79. VHF blade antenna.
80. Identification antenna.
81. Six abreast tourist seating (16-in. aisle—78 seats).
82. Radiant heating panels.
83. Inner skin.
84. Anti-collision light.
85. Starboard rear galley service door (64 in. x 37 in.).
86. Aft galley.
87. Dished-type stringers, aft compartment area only.
88. Cabin air pressure relief valve.
89. Rear plug type entry door (72 in. x 34 in.).
90. Attendant's seats.
91. Toilets (three).

92. Clothes closet.
93. Aft pressure bulkhead.

TAIL UNIT

94. Elevator control cables.
95. Rudder servo cables.
96. Aft galley and toilet water supply tank (20 U.S. gals. each).
97. Integral three-spar fin.
98. Fin to rear fuselage attachment points.
99. Rear fuselage sloping frames.
100. Channel sectioned stringers.
101. HF antenna coupler unit.
102. Horizontal stabilizer actuator.
103. Reinforcing plate.
104. Rudder power actuator.
105. Rudder tab linkage.

Jet set

The 'swinging sixties' was one of the most defining decades in history. It was a time of cultural revolution in social norms about clothing, music, drugs, sexuality and formalities.

As the British economy recovered after the austerity of the 1950s, London embraced the new-found freedom and business at Heathrow boomed. At the time, the airport resounded to jets adorned with either 'BOAC blue' or 'BEA red', but carriers from around the world also gave it a very cosmopolitan feel. As new generations of jets appeared, the stands at Heathrow offered an exotic array of types, some of which are featured in this chapter. And it was not just the aircraft that drew the spectators by the thousands, there was always the chance of bumping in to a famous celebrity…

This spread: **A true child of the sixties, the Douglas DC-8 was a four-engine long-range narrow-body jet airliner that was a competitor to Boeing's all-conquering 707. Most DC-8s were powered by Pratt& Whitney engines, but 32 were built as the Series 40 which were fitted with Rolls-Royce Conway 509 turbojets (left). Dutch carrier KLM was an early user of the DC-8 and Series 33 PH-DCC was christened 'Sir Frank Whittle' by the man himself during a ceremony at the north side of Heathrow.**

Fab four

Right: The one time that human decibel levels rivalled those of the jets. The Beatles first tour to America in 1964 attracted more than 5,000 fans to wave them off from Heathrow. The frenzied scenes were only beaten when the 'Fab Four' arrived back and the airport was almost brought to a standstill.

Top right: The Rolling Stones, minus lead singer Mick Jagger, pictured at London's Heathrow Airport en route to the US in September 1967.

Bottom right: Looking as chic as ever, the French film actress Brigitte Bardot disembarks from an Air France Caravelle in November 1967.

Below: The epitome of 'cool', Steve McQueen heading from Heathrow to Paris for Le Mans in April 1970.

*Left: **The Sud-Aviation SE210 Caravelles of Air France were a regular sight at Heathrow as they plied the lucrative Paris to London network. The SE210 made its maiden flight in 1955 and featured a nose and cockpit area taken directly from the Comet. Its unique triangular windows were to remain a distinctive feature throughout its career. In total, 282 Caravelles were built.***

*Right: **A four-engined airliner regularly seen at Heathrow were the Convair 990 Coronados of Swissair. The airline bought eight Convair 990As beginning in 1962, operating them on long-distance routes to South America, West Africa, the Middle and Far East, as well as on European routes with heavy traffic. Their fleet was withdrawn from service in 1975. The 990's niche was soon captured by the Boeing 720 and Boeing 720B, derivatives of the Boeing 707, and later by the Boeing 727. By the time the assembly line shut down in 1963, only 37 had been produced and sightings were rare.***

Right and far right: **History was made on 22 March 1956 when the Soviet Tu-104 prototype, CCCP L5400, arrived at London Heathrow carrying Soviet Col-Gen Ivan Serov, and other Soviet officials (far right). Just over three years later, Tupolev Tu-104A CCCP-42382 inaugurated the Moscow -London service, with BEA Viscounts looking on.**

Below: **The angular profile of Tupolev Tu-134 OK-CFC of CSA (Czechoslovak State Airlines) at Heathrow Airport in the early 1970s. A total of 854 of the twin-engined airliner was built in the Soviet Union from 1966 to 1984, with Aeroflot being the largest user.**

CCCP-42382

Esso
ESSO AVIATION PRODUCTS

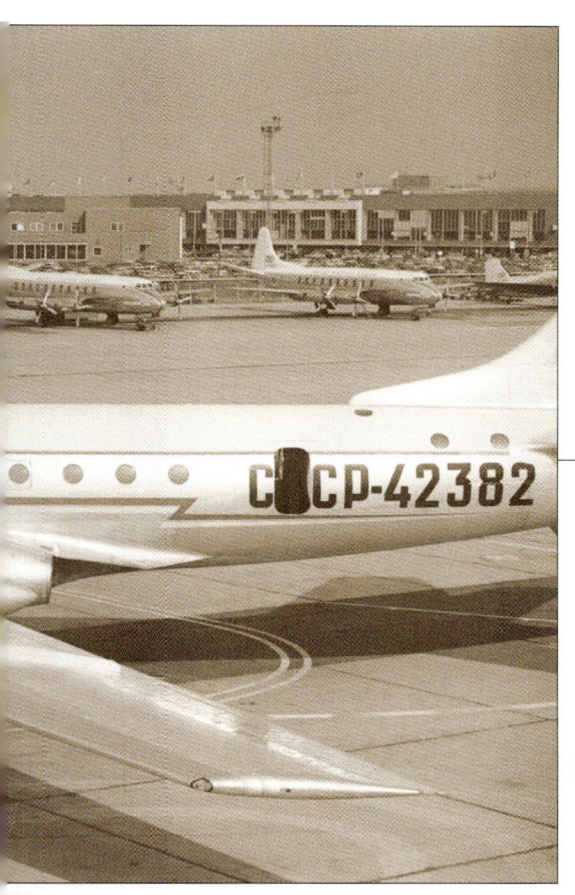

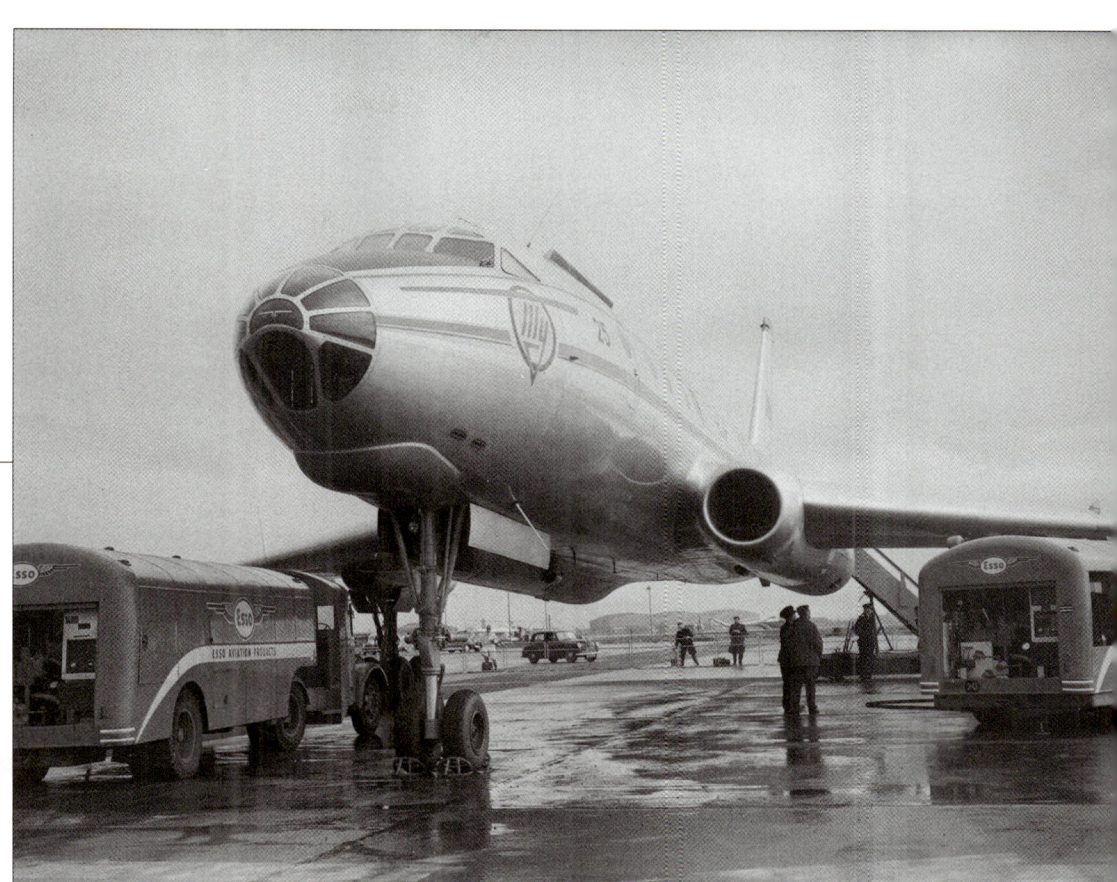

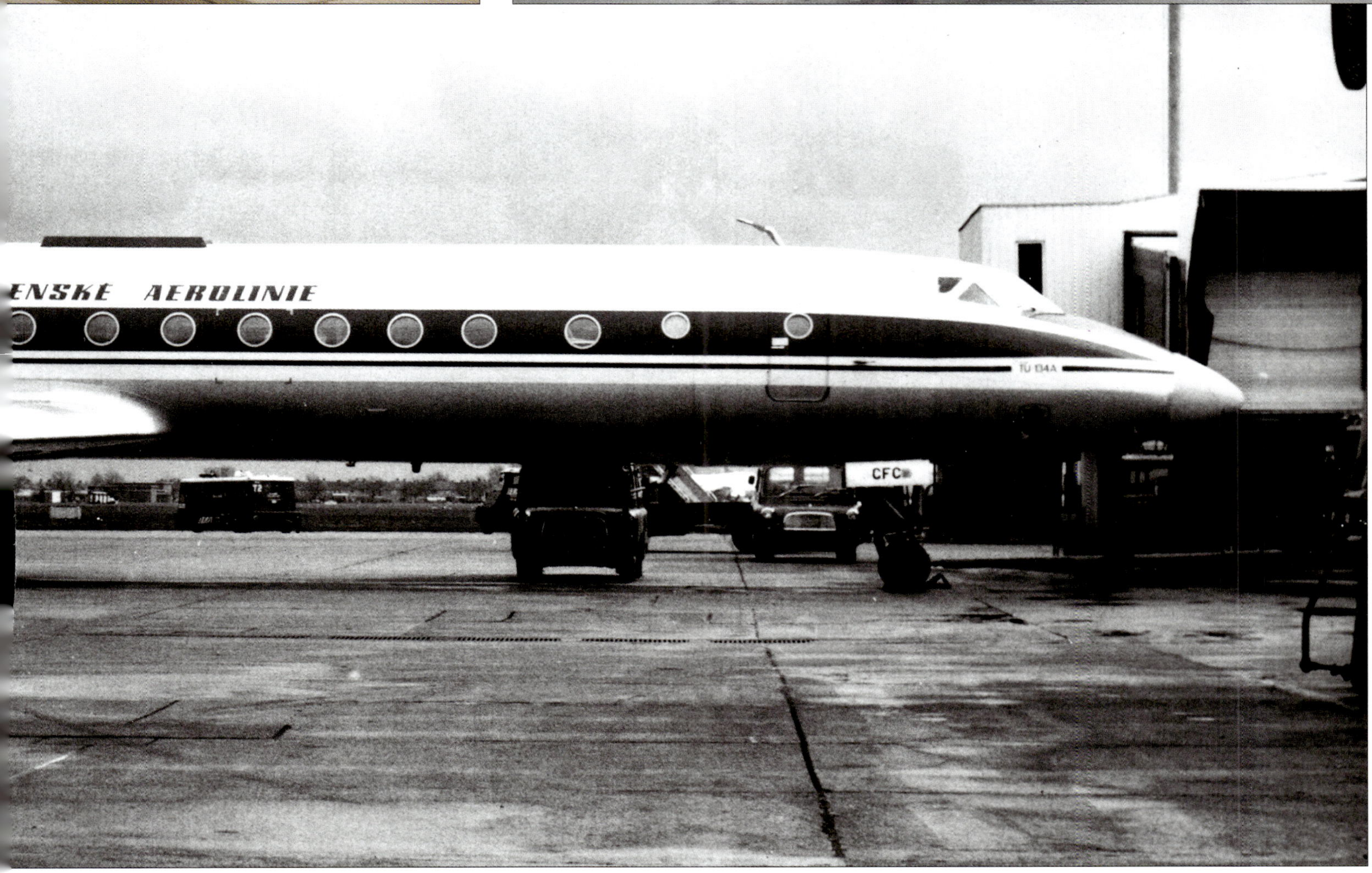
ENSKE AEROLINIE
TU 134A
CFC

Ten out of ten

I f ever an airliner looked 'right', it was the VC10. Its slender fuselage was graced by elegantly swept wings and an even more elegant T-tail. But sadly looks aren't everything and this icon of the skies did not achieve the success that it deserved.

BOAC issued a requirement in 1957 for a Comet and Britannia replacement with specifications tailored to its Middle-East and African routes. Vickers responded with what was to become the VC10, a sleek futuristic airliner with accommodation for about 135 passengers in a BOAC two class layout (or up to 151 all economy class) in a six abreast

cabin. Powered by four Rolls-Royce Conways mounted in pairs on either side of the rear fuselage, it featured a T-tail (both of these a first for a large jet transport). In order to meet the stringent runway requirements, it was fitted with a very efficient wing with leading edge slats, outboard ailerons, upper wing spoilers and massive Fowler flaps.

The initial model (which later became known as the 'Standard') was ordered in several versions, not only by BOAC but also by Ghana Airways, Nigeria Airways, British United Airways and the RAF. Studies into a higher capacity version of the VC10

*Top: **One of the first 'standard' VC10s delivered to BOAC was G-ARVF . Even on the ground the VC10 had near perfect proportions.***

*Inset: **BOAC's smart and classic livery sat beautifully on the Vickers VC10, as modelled by G-ARVI.** Andy Hay/Flyingart.co.uk*

were instigated early in the development programme. The philosophy behind what emerged as the Type 1150 Super VC10 was to provide extra seating capacity at the expense of some of the Standard VC10's 'hot and high' airfield performance. Where the Standard VC10 was optimised for BOAC's routes into

the demanding airfields of the Middle East, Far East and Africa, the stretched Super was intended to provide more economical operation (especially in the case of seat/mile costs) on other major routes including the important North Atlantic.

BOAC eventually settled on 12 Standards and 17 Supers, considerably less than the original 35 orders plus 20 options, the first of which entered service on 29 April 1964. Amongst the cancellations were eight Supers, which would have been built as a mixed passenger/freighter version with the large cargo door that had been developed for the

Standard. This version eventually did fly as East African Airways bought five Type 1154s. The total production run eventually totalled out at 32 aircraft for the Standard and 22 for the Super, not a particularly impressive number, but in its time the VC10 was the largest aircraft that had ever been produced in the UK. In the end it had been tailored too much to meet BOAC's demands and it was not able to challenge the domination of the Boeing 707 and DC-8.

Passengers loved the VC10. Not only did it look the part, but its rear-mounted engines and beautifully swept wing meant that it was

very quiet and gave a very smooth ride. After only six months of operating the Super VC10 on the North Atlantic routes, BOAC had seen their average passenger load increase by 40% compared to the same service with Boeing 707s.

In the end the passenger appeal of the VC10 didn't save it. The Standards were quickly withdrawn from use in 1974 when BOAC decided that they were no longer economically viable, especially with the 747 rendering the type superfluous to requirements. The Supers soldiered on for another six years with the final Super flight in BOAC (by then actually British Airways) service in March 1981.

This picture: The performance of the Super VC10 was such that it achieved the fastest crossing of the Atlantic by a jet airliner, a record still held to date for a sub-sonic airliner, of 5hrs 1min.

Below: T-tails galore on the apron at Heathrow. Sadly this sight was not as common as Vickers would have liked.

Below right: The 'Combi' version of the VC10 was only operated by East African Airways. Of its five examples, one was destroyed in a take-off accident at Addis Ababa in 1972, and the other four were retired in 1977 and returned to BAC, subsequently being purchased by the RAF. 5H-MOG had the distinction of being the last VC10 built.

'Jumbo' arrival

There were many defining moments in Heathrow's first 25 years of operation, but arguably the most significant was the arrival of the first Boeing 747. Representing a quantum leap in airliner capacity, the game-changing giant brought worldwide travel to the masses.

'A luxurious auditorium some genie has wafted aloft.' This was how a Times reporter heralded the arrival of the first Boeing 747 at Heathrow. A BBC news reporter was less prosaic and more factual in his bulletin: 'The newly-constructed Boeing 747, Pan Am Flight Two, touched down at Heathrow at 14.14GMT today – seven hours late due to technical problems. The jumbo had brought 324 passengers across the Atlantic from New York to London. But the return journey to New York did not run so smoothly. Thirty-six of the 153 passengers transferred to other flights after a faulty compressed air bottle, used to blow open the plane's door in an emergency, meant take-off was delayed for four-and-a-half hours at Heathrow. In spite of these problems it is thought the 360-seat 747, now the largest aeroplane on the market, will herald the dawn of a new era in long-distance air travel for a huge number of travellers.'

By 1966 it was apparent that if BOAC was to remain competitive on the North Atlantic routes, it would have to join Pan American and TWA in ordering the giant Boeing 747 and by 1968 it had eight on order at a cost of £165.5 million. BOAC's first 747, G-AWNA, was delivered on 23 May 1970, but a pilot's dispute delayed the inauguration of Boeing 747 services with the carrier for nearly a year, with the first three standing idle at Heathrow. Eventually the inaugural BOAC Boeing 747 service took place on 14 April 1971, from London to New York. The introduction of the 747 brought about a quantum leap in airliner size (roughly two and a half times the capacity of a B707) and Heathrow had to adapt to handle the jets. Accordingly, in February 1968 the BAA announced its plans for coping with the influx of Boeing 747s. It was proposed to close Runway 33L/15R and build a new pier system starting at the Oceanic Building and ending in a series of forward

*Below: **One of the first Boeing 747s to be received by Pan Am was N743PA, seen here about to defy gravity. For good reason, the majestic Boeing was often referred to as 'Queen of the Skies'.***

*Right: **The first Boeing 747 to operate scheduled commercial services is notable for its brief but significant history. In its first year of service, N736PA 'Clipper Young America' became the first 747 to be hijacked, when it was flown to Cuba on 2 August 1970. Following this incident, it was renamed 'Clipper Victor', but was later destroyed in the world's deadliest aviation accident at the Tenerife airport disaster, when a KLM Boeing 747 attempted to take off without clearance, colliding with 'Clipper Victor' on the runway.***

lounges on the site of the runway. A new long-haul arrivals building was to be built adjacent to the Oceanic Building. The whole long-haul terminal complex was to be renamed Terminal 3.

Within six months of launch, the Boeing 747 had carried a million passengers and within a year nearly 100 were being operated by 17 airlines and the number of passengers had increased to seven million.

The world domination of the Boeing 747 had begun and with it the airliner industry had been changed forever.

*Right: **When TWA launched its New York–London route with the Boeing 747 in 1970, they celebrated by crowning a 7-year-old British girl 'Little Miss Superjet'.***

*Below: **Pan Am was the first airline to fly the Queen of the Skies. Here, Pan Am flight attendants celebrate the arrival of the Boeing 747 at London's Heathrow Airport for the first time.***

*Bottom: **BOAC's first Boeing 747 on arrival at Heathrow on 23 May 1970. However, owing to a pilot's dispute the carrier was not able to commence wide-body service until a year later.***

Luxury in the air

Above: **The first-class cabin on the main deck of a Pan Am 747.**

Right: **BOAC first-class passengers enjoy a champagne lunch on board one of its first Boeing 747 transatlantic services.**

Below: **Inside a Pan Am Boeing 747's upper deck, with a bar and comfortable seating where passengers could relax, drink and smoke, during the flight.**

Heathrow timeline 1945-1970

May 1945:	When World War Two ends, the new airfield is still under construction. By then, the plans have already changed from tenuous wartime military use to overt development into an international airport.
1 January 1946:	Ownership of the site is transferred from the Air Ministry to the Ministry of Civil Aviation.
10 January 1946:	The British Cabinet agrees Stage 3 of the airport, which is an extension north of the Bath Road, with a large triangle of three runways, obliterating Sipson and most of Harlington and diverting the Bath Road.
25 March 1946:	Lord Winster, the Minister of Aviation, performs the official opening ceremony of the newly named London Airport. The first aircraft to use the new airport is a British South American Airways (BSAA) Avro Lancastrian named 'Star Light'. The passenger terminal is an area of Army tents and duckboarding next to the south side of the Bath Road. The first control tower is a crude brick building.
16 April 1946:	The first aircraft of a foreign airline, a Panair Lockheed 049 Constellation, lands after a flight from Rio de Janeiro. BOAC's first scheduled flight is an Avro Lancastrian heading for Australia on a route operated jointly with Qantas.
1947:	By now Heathrow's runways form a triangle consisting of 10/28 (9,200ft long), 15/33 (6,300ft) and 52/23 (6,700ft) long. A parallel runway farther west soon replaces 15/33 thereby expanding the planned terminal area inside the triangle. The temporary 'prefab' passenger and cargo buildings are at the northeast edge of the airport, just south of Bath Road.
Early 1950s:	Three more runways are completed to make a rough hexagram arrangement within which two runways would always be within 30° of the wind direction.
31 October 1950:	BEA Vickers Viking crashes in thick fog.
7 February 1952:	Princess Elizabeth returns to the UK as Queen Elizabeth II. She arrives on the BOAC Argonaut 'Atalanta'.
2 May 1952:	A de Havilland Comet of BOAC becomes the first jet airliner to enter commercial service.
December 1953:	Plans to expand north of the Bath Road are abandoned, to great local rejoicing.
December 1953:	Passenger traffic reaches 1 million, with a total of 62,000 flights completed over the year.
1955:	Queen Elizabeth II opens the first permanent passenger terminal, the Europa Building, later known as Terminal 2. These terminal buildings stand in the central area in the middle of the star pattern of runways and are reached by a twin access tunnel from the Bath Road (A4) passing under Runway 28R/10L .

1 April 1955: A striking new 127ft –high (38.8m) control tower designed by Frederick Gibberd opens to replace the original 1940s tower.

Late 1950s: BEA Helicopters runs an experimental helicopter service to Heathrow Central from London's South Bank and other destinations. The Roof Gardens on top of the Queen's Building and Europa Terminal become very popular with the public.

1955: The first central terminal building is named Building 1 Europa.

1956: The second central terminal building (linked to Building 1) is named Building 2 Britannic.

3 October 1958: A BOAC Comet 4 operates the first non-stop transatlantic jet service from New York-London.

13 November 1961: The Oceanic Terminal (renamed as Terminal 3 in 1968) is opened to handle long-haul flight departures.

1964: The legal dispute between Fairey Aviation and the government over compensation, which started in early 1944, is finally settled. Fairey's 1930 hangar, in legal limbo for 20 years, and used as the Heathrow Airport fire station and as backdrop for an advertising billboard for BOAC, is finally demolished.

1966: London Airport is renamed Heathrow.

May 1968: Terminal 1 opens, completing the cluster of buildings at the centre of the airport site. By this time Heathrow is handling 14 million passengers annually.

6 April 1968: BOAC Flight 712 operated by a Boeing 707-465 from London to Sydney suffers an engine failure on take-off. The engine falls off in flight and the aircraft makes a successful emergency landing, but is consumed by flames. Five people die.

May 1969: Queen Elizabeth II formally inaugurates Terminal 1.

Late 1960s: The cargo terminal is built to the south of the southern runway, connected to Terminals 1, 2 and 3 by the Heathrow Cargo Tunnel.

1970: Terminal 3 is expanded with the addition of an arrivals building in 1970. Other new facilities include the UK's first moving walkways. Heathrow's two main east-west runways, 10L/28R and 10R/28L (later redesignated 09L/27R and 09R/27L) are also extended to their current lengths to accommodate new large jets such as the Boeing 747. The other runways are closed to facilitate terminal expansion, except for Runway 23, which remained available for crosswind landings until 2002.

22 January 1970: The first wide-body Boeing 747 scheduled service operated by Pan Am lands at Heathrow, heralding the start of a new era.